SUSAN B.
ANTHONY

AMERICAN WOMEN of ACHIEVEMENT

SUSAN B. ANTHONY

BARBARA WEISBERG

CHELSEA HOUSE PUBLISHERS

NEW YORK • PHILADELPHIA

Chelsea House Publishers

EDITOR-IN-CHIEF: Nancy Toff
EXECUTIVE EDITOR: Remmel T. Nunn
MANAGING EDITOR: Karyn Gullen Browne
COPY CHIEF: Juliann Barbato
PICTURE EDITOR: Adrian G. Allen
ART DIRECTOR: Giannella Garrett
MANUFACTURING MANAGER: Gerald Levine

American Women of Achievement
SENIOR EDITOR: Constance Jones

Staff for Susan B. Anthony

TEXT EDITOR: Marian W. Taylor
COPY EDITOR: Karen Hammonds
DEPUTY COPY CHIEF: Ellen Scordato
EDITORIAL ASSISTANT: Theodore Keyes
PICTURE RESEARCHER: Faith Schornick, Joan Beard
DESIGN: Design Oasis
ASSISTANT DESIGNER: Donna Sinisgalli
PRODUCTION COORDINATOR: Joseph Romano
COVER ILLUSTRATOR: Bradford Brown

7   9   8   6

Library of Congress Cataloging in Publication Data

Weisberg, Barbara.
   Susan B. Anthony

(American women of achievement)
Bibliography: p.
Includes index.
Summary: A biography of an early leader in the campaign for
women's rights, particularly in getting women the right to vote.
1. Anthony, Susan B. (Susan Brownell), 1820–1906—Juvenile
literature.   2. Feminists—United States—Biography—Juvenile
literature.   3. Suffragettes—United States—Biography—Juvenile
literature. [1. Anthony, Susan B. (Susan Brownell),
1820–1906. 2. Feminists] I. Title. II. Series.

HQ1413.A55W45   1988   324.6'23'0924 [B] [92]   87-35528

ISBN 1-55546-639-7
   0-7910-0408-2 (pbk.)

CONTENTS

AMERICAN WOMEN of ACHIEVEMENT

Abigail Adams
women's rights advocate

Jane Addams
social worker

Louisa May Alcott
author

Marian Anderson
singer

Susan B. Anthony
woman suffragist

Ethel Barrymore
actress

Clara Barton
founder of the American Red Cross

Elizabeth Blackwell
physician

Nellie Bly
journalist

Margaret Bourke-White
photographer

Pearl Buck
author

Rachel Carson
biologist and author

Mary Cassatt
artist

Agnes De Mille
choreographer

Emily Dickinson
poet

Isadora Duncan
dancer

Amelia Earhart
aviator

Mary Baker Eddy
founder of the Christian Science church

Betty Friedan
feminist

Althea Gibson
tennis champion

Emma Goldman
political activist

Helen Hayes
actress

Lillian Hellman
playwright

Katharine Hepburn
actress

Karen Horney
psychoanalyst

Anne Hutchinson
religious leader

Mahalia Jackson
gospel singer

Helen Keller
humanitarian

Jeane Kirkpatrick
diplomat

Emma Lazarus
poet

Clare Boothe Luce
author and diplomat

Barbara McClintock
biologist

Margaret Mead
anthropologist

Edna St. Vincent Millay
poet

Julia Morgan
architect

Grandma Moses
painter

Louise Nevelson
sculptor

Sandra Day O'Connor
Supreme Court justice

Georgia O'Keeffe
painter

Eleanor Roosevelt
diplomat and humanitarian

Wilma Rudolph
champion athlete

Florence Sabin
medical researcher

Beverly Sills
opera singer

Gertrude Stein
author

Gloria Steinem
feminist

Harriet Beecher Stowe
author and abolitionist

Mae West
entertainer

Edith Wharton
author

Phillis Wheatley
poet

Babe Didrikson Zaharias
champion athlete

CHELSEA HOUSE PUBLISHERS

"Remember the Ladies"

MATINA S. HORNER

Remember the Ladies." That is what Abigail Adams wrote to her husband John, then a delegate to the Continental Congress, as the Founding Fathers met in Philadelphia to form a new nation in March of 1776. "Be more generous and favorable to them than your ancestors. Do not put such unlimited power in the hands of the Husbands. If particular care and attention is not paid to the Ladies," Abigail Adams warned, "we are determined to foment a Rebellion, and will not hold ourselves bound by any Laws in which we have no voice, or Representation."

The words of Abigail Adams, one of the earliest American advocates of women's rights, were prophetic. Because when we have not "remembered the ladies," they have, by their words and deeds, reminded us so forcefully of the omission that we cannot fail to remember them. For the history of American women is as interesting and varied as the history of our nation as a whole. American women have played an integral part in founding, settling, and building our country. Some we remember as remarkable women who— against great odds—achieved distinction in the public arena: Anne Hutchinson, who in the 17th century became a charismatic religious leader; Phillis Wheatley, an 18th-century black slave who became a poet; Susan B. Anthony, whose name is synonymous with the 19th-century women's rights movement, and who led the struggle to enfranchise women; and, in our own century, Amelia Earhart, the first woman to cross the Atlantic Ocean by air.

These extraordinary women certainly merit our admiration, but other women, "common women," many of them all but forgotten, should also be recognized for their contributions to American thought and culture. Women have been community builders; they have founded schools and formed voluntary associations to help those in need; they have assumed the major responsibility for rearing children, passing on from one generation to the next the values that keep a culture alive. These and innumerable other contributions, once ignored, are now being recognized by scholars, students, and the public. It is exciting and gratifying to realize that a part of our history that was hardly acknowledged a few generations ago is now being studied and brought to light.

In recent decades, the field of women's history has grown from obscurity to a politically controversial splinter movement to academic respectability, in many cases mainstreamed into such traditional disciplines as history, economics, and psychology. Scholars of women, both female and male, have organized research centers at such prestigious institutions as Wellesley College, Stanford University, and the University of California. Other notable centers for women's studies are the Center for the American Woman and Politics at the Eagleton Institute of Politics at Rutgers University; the Henry A. Murray Research Center for the Study of Lives, at Radcliffe College; and the Women's Research and Education Institute, the research arm of the Congressional Caucus on Women's Issues. Other scholars and public figures have established archives and libraries, such as the Schlesinger Library on the History of Women in America, at Radcliffe College, and the Sophia Smith Collection, at Smith College, to collect and preserve the written and tangible legacies of women.

From the initial donation of the Women's Rights Collection in 1943, the Schlesinger Library grew to encompass vast collections documenting the manifold accomplishments of American women. Simultaneously, the women's movement in general and the academic discipline of women's studies in particular also began with a narrow definition and gradually expanded their mandate. Early causes such as woman suffrage and social reform, abolition and organized labor were joined by newer concerns such as the history of women in business and the professions and in politics and government; the study of the family; and social issues such as health policy and education.

Women, as historian Arthur M. Schlesinger, jr., once pointed out, "have constituted the most spectacular casualty of traditional history. They have made up at least half the human race, but you could never tell that by looking at the books historians write." The new breed of historians is remedying that omission. They have written books about immigrant women and about work-ing-class women who struggled for survival in cities and about black women who met the challenges of life in rural areas. They are telling the stories of women who, despite the barriers of tradition and economics, became lawyers and doctors and public figures.

The women's studies movement has also led scholars to question tradi-tional interpretations of their respective disciplines. For example, the study of war has traditionally been an exercise in military and political analysis, an examination of strategies planned and executed by men. But scholars of women's history have pointed out that wars have also been periods of tre-mendous change and even opportunity for women, because the very absence of men on the home front enabled them to expand their educational, eco-nomic, and professional activities and to assume leadership in their homes.

The early scholars of women's history showed a unique brand of courage in choosing to investigate new subjects and take new approaches to old ones. Often, like their subjects, they endured criticism and even ostracism by their academic colleagues. But their efforts have unquestionably been worthwhile, because with the publication of each new study and book another piece of the historical patchwork is sewn into place, revealing an increasingly com-prehensive picture of the role of women in our rich and varied history.

Such books on groups of women are essential, but books that focus on the lives of individuals are equally indispensable. Biographies can be inspirational, offering their readers the example of people with vision who have looked outside themselves for their goals and have often struggled against great obstacles to achieve them. Marian Anderson, for instance, had to overcome racial bigotry in order to perfect her art and perform as a concert singer. Isadora Duncan defied the rules of classical dance to find true artistic free-dom. Jane Addams had to break down society's notions of the proper role for women in order to create new social institutions, notably the settlement house. All of these women had to come to terms both with themselves and with the world in which they lived. Only then could they move ahead as pioneers in their chosen callings.

Biography can inspire not only by adulation but also by realism. It helps us to see not only the qualities in others that we hope to emulate, but also, perhaps, the weaknesses that made them "human." By helping us identify with the subject on a more personal level they help us to feel that we, too, can achieve such goals. We read about Eleanor Roosevelt, for instance, who occupied a unique and seemingly enviable position as the wife of the pres-ident. Yet we can sympathize with her inner dilemma: an inherently shy woman, she had to force herself to live a most public life in order to use her position to benefit others. We may not be able to imagine ourselves having the immense poetic talent of Emily Dickinson, but from her story we can understand the challenges faced by a creative woman who was expected to fulfill many family responsibilities. And though few of us will ever reach the level of athletic accomplishment displayed by Wilma Rudolph or Babe Zaharias, we can still appreciate their spirit, their overwhelming will to excel.

A biography is a multifaceted lens. It is first of all a magnification, the intimate examination of one particular life. But at the same time, it is a wide-angle lens, informing us about the world in which the subject lived. We come away from reading about one life knowing more about the social, political, and economic fabric of the time. It is for this reason, perhaps, that the great New England essayist Ralph Waldo Emerson wrote, in 1841, "There is properly no history: only biography." And it is also why biography, and particularly women's biography, will continue to fascinate writers and readers alike.

SUSAN B. ANTHONY

*Susan B. Anthony was 52 years old when she was arrested for voting illegally in 1872;
she would spend another 3 decades battling for woman suffrage.*

ONE

Arrest and Trial

On November 18, 1872, in Rochester, New York, E. J. Keeney was nervous. As a deputy U.S. marshal, he had made many arrests, but this one was different. His steps slowed as he approached the brick house at 7 Madison Street. Finally, he climbed the steps, took a deep breath, and rang the bell. When the door opened, he removed his hat and asked for Miss Susan B. Anthony. Identifying herself as Anthony, the tall, silver-haired woman at the door asked the visitor what he wanted. He was there, he stammered, to arrest her.

Anthony, she later told an interviewer, asked, "Is this your usual method of serving a warrant?" Keeney quickly reached into his pocket and produced a document. It charged Anthony with a crime: voting "for a representative in the Congress of the United States, without having a lawful right to vote." It was Keeney's duty to bring the accused to the office of the U.S. commissioner of elections in Rochester, but, he hastily explained, she could go alone whenever she was ready.

Anthony said she would not think of going by herself, and dramatically extended her hands for handcuffs. Ignoring the invitation, the embarrassed Keeney escorted his prisoner out of the house and down to the corner, where he helped her board a streetcar. When the conductor asked for her fare, her response, she recalled later, could be heard at the back of the car. "I'm traveling at the expense of the government," she said. "This gentleman is escorting me to jail. Ask him for my

13

fare." Keeney meekly deposited the money, and the pair rode to the office of the commissioner.

In the 1870s, most prosperous, middle-aged American women would have been mortified to find themselves in Anthony's situation. Susan B. An-

This redbrick house in Rochester, New York, was the scene of Anthony's arrest by U.S. deputy marshal E. J. Keeney on November 18, 1872.

thony, however, was not a typical Victorian "lady." She had indeed voted illegally, and she had done it for a reason. A pioneer in the movement to achieve full civil rights for women, she had spent the past 20 years campaigning for woman suffrage (women's right to vote). She had carried her message through blizzards, spoken before jeering crowds, and withstood withering scorn from pulpit and press. Nothing had kept her from demanding equal rights for men and women. Now she was prepared to face a trial and possible jail sentence.

Women were forbidden by law to vote in New York (or any other) State. Anthony had challenged the law when she cast her ballot in 1872. She had planned to bring a court case against Rochester's election inspectors if her vote was discounted. She had not expected to be arrested, but now that she was in custody, she hoped to use the occasion to make a point.

Along with other suffragists, both male and female, Anthony believed that the U.S. Constitution gave women the right to vote. The Fourteenth Amendment, ratified amid intense controversy in 1868, had been designed to guarantee black men the same rights as white men. Although it specifically discussed the right to vote of *male* citizens, it also stated that "All persons born or naturalized in the United States . . . are citizens of the United States." And the Fifteenth

An 1870 lithograph celebrates passage of the Constitution's Fifteenth Amendment, which confirmed the right of black men—but neither black nor white women—to vote.

Amendment, passed in 1870, said, "The right of citizens of the United States to vote shall not be denied or abridged . . . on account of race, color, or previous condition of servitude [slavery]."

Because citizens could not be denied the vote, and because women were citizens, it seemed self-evident to the suffragists that women had the right to vote. Conservatives, however, held that the right to vote had always been limited to men, and that because the words "race, color, or previous condition of servitude" clearly referred

to blacks, the amendments applied only to black men. In the 1870s, as for the next half-century, such conservatives would retain control of the U.S. government, and voting women would be considered lawbreakers.

In the early 1870s, almost 100 American women had unsuccessfully tried to register and vote. Anthony, who had been urging women to claim their voting rights under the Fourteenth and Fifteenth Amendments, had been waiting her own turn. Anticipating the national election of November 5, 1872, she spent 30 days in Rochester, fulfill-

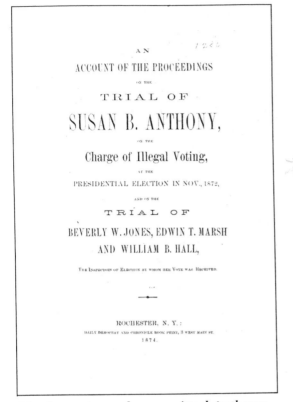

AN
ACCOUNT OF THE PROCEEDINGS
ON THE
TRIAL OF
SUSAN B. ANTHONY,
ON THE
Charge of Illegal Voting,
AT THE
PRESIDENTIAL ELECTION IN NOV., 1872,
AND ON THE
TRIAL OF
BEVERLY W. JONES, EDWIN T. MARSH
AND WILLIAM B. HALL,
THE INSPECTORS OF ELECTION BY WHOM HER VOTE WAS RECEIVED.

ROCHESTER, N. Y.:
DAILY DEMOCRAT AND CHRONICLE BOOK PRINT, 3 WEST MAIN ST.
1874.

The inspectors who permitted Anthony to vote were also tried and found guilty. Fined $25 each, the 3 men were later pardoned by President Ulysses S. Grant.

ing the minimum term of legal residence. On the morning of November 1, she and her three sisters marched into the barbershop where the local men had gathered to register.

When the women demanded to be registered themselves, the election inspector told them that under the law of New York State, women could not vote. Anthony explained that she and her sisters claimed their right to vote on the basis of the Constitution, which superseded state laws. Then she read sections from the controversial amendments. Suprisingly, the inspector backed down and allowed the women to register. The news spread among Rochester's feminist activists, resulting in the registration of another eight women.

On November 5, Anthony cast her first ballot. She reported the event in a letter to her good friend and fellow suffragist leader, Elizabeth Cady Stanton: "Well, I have been and gone and done it, positively voted this morning at 7 o'clock, and swore my vote in at that. Not a jeer, not a rude word, not a disrespectful look has met one woman. Now if all our suffrage women would work to this end ... what strides we might make from now on!"

Less than two weeks later, Marshal Keeney knocked at Anthony's door with his arrest warrant. Anthony's hearing was held in a small courtroom that had once been used for trials of runaway slaves. During the hearing, the elections commissioner asked Anthony if she had any doubt of her right to vote. "Not a particle," she replied.

After she was indicted, the judge set a trial date for the following spring. The indictment asserted that as "a person of the female sex," she had "knowingly, wrongfully, and unlawfully voted ... contrary to the form of the statute and against the peace of the United States of America."

This mocking newspaper cartoon, entitled "The Woman Who Dared," appeared after Anthony's 1873 conviction for "voting without a lawful right to vote."

Male election inspectors gesture dismissively as New York City suffragists, following Anthony's well-publicized example, attempt to cast ballots in 1875.

Anthony said of the case, "The one question to be settled is, are personal freedom and personal representation inherent rights and privileges? Or are they things ... to be given and taken [by] ... a ruling class or a majority vote? If the former, then is our country free indeed; if the latter, then is our country a despotism, and we women its victims!"

Released on bail, Anthony set off on a whirlwind tour of speaking engagements and meetings. As she prepared to leave from the Rochester train station in January, she saw Marshal Kee-ney pacing up and down the platform. She was still technically in his custody, and, as she noted in her diary, he "quite protested against my going." Apparently still embarrassed about treating this dignified woman as a prisoner, however, Keeney made no move to stop her. But during the months preceding the trial, she never boarded a train without seeing the marshal at the station.

During the next few months, Anthony lectured in Ohio, Indiana, and Illinois, as well as in many cities in New York. Wherever she went, she told the story of her arrest and pending trial. Over and over, she carefully explained the legal points of the Fourteenth and Fifteenth Amendments that she believed justified her vote.

Anthony often paraphrased the Constitution in her speeches. "It was we, the people, not we, the white male citizens, nor yet we, the male citizens: but we the whole people, who formed this Union," she said. "And we formed it . . . to give the blessings of liberty . . . to the whole people—women as well as men."

In part because Anthony's arrest had received extensive newspaper coverage, her speeches drew large audiences. A powerful speaker, she was also an imposing physical presence on the lecture platform. Describing her appearance, one reporter wrote, "Miss Anthony was fashionably dressed in black silk . . . with flowing sleeves, heavily trimmed in black lace; ruffled white undersleeves and a broad, graceful lace collar, with a gold neck chain and pendant. Her abundant hair was brushed back and bound in a knot after the fashion of our grandmothers."

Press reaction to Anthony's campaign was mixed. Some newspapers published mocking stories and cartoons that showed her as a fierce, umbrella-wielding "old maid," but others were supportive. The *Rochester Express*, for example, called her "a refined and estimable woman, thoroughly respected and beloved by the large circle of staunch friends who swear by her common sense and loyalty, if not by her peculiar views." One Rochester woman was quoted as saying, "No, I am not converted to what [the suffragists] advocate. I am too cowardly for that; but I am converted to Susan B. Anthony."

On June 17, 1873, Anthony was brought to trial before Ward Hunt, a judge well known for his strong anti-feminist views. His first move was to deny Anthony the right to testify in her own behalf. Speaking for her was lawyer Henry Selden, who argued that his client was on trial simply for being a woman. "If the same act had been done by her brother," he said, "the act would have been . . . honorable, but having been done by a woman, it is said to be a crime. . . . I believe this is the first instance in which a woman has been arraigned in a criminal court merely on account of her sex."

After the lawyer had concluded his remarks, the judge read the jury a statement he had written before the trial even began. "The 14th Amendment," he asserted, "gives no right to a woman to vote, and the voting of Miss Anthony was in violation of the law." Hunt then directed the jury "to find a vote of guilty." Selden leaped to his feet in protest. It was, he insisted, up to the jury to determine Anthony's guilt or innocence. Ignoring him, Hunt ordered the court clerk to record a verdict of guilty, even though the jury had

Male allies of the woman-suffrage movement are lampooned in an 1869 Currier and Ives print. Its caption reads, "The Age of Iron: Man As He Expects to Be."

not voted. Then, over Selden's continued objections, he said, "Gentlemen of the jury, you are discharged."

Arguing that Anthony had been denied her right to trial by jury, Selden asked for a new trial, but the judge denied the motion. The next day, Anthony stood before Hunt as he said, "Has the prisoner anything to say why sentence should not be pronounced?" This was Anthony's long-awaited opportunity, and her voice rang out.

"Yes, your honor, I have many things to say," she said. "You have trampled underfoot every vital principle of our government. My natural rights, my civil rights, my political rights, my judicial rights, are all alike ignored." Over the judge's continued demands for her silence, Anthony kept on talking. At last, Hunt's voice drowned hers. "The prisoner," he insisted, "has been tried according to established forms of law."

"Yes, your honor," she shot back, "but by forms of law all made by men, interpreted by men, administered by men, in favor of men and against women."

By now, the judge was shouting. "The court orders the prisoner to sit down," he thundered. "It will not allow another word!" When Anthony halted

at last, Hunt delivered her sentence: a fine of $100 plus court costs.

Anthony responded in a controlled voice. "May it please your honor," she said, "I shall never pay a dollar of your unjust penalty." Furthermore, she said, "I shall earnestly and persistently

continue to urge all women to the practical recognition of the old revolutionary maxim that 'Resistance to tyranny is obedience to God.' "

If Hunt had imprisoned Anthony for refusing to pay the fine, her case might have been carried into the U.S. Supreme Court. Foreseeing such a possibility, the judge announced he would not send her to prison. By freeing her, he closed the case for good. His actions, wrote a furious Anthony in her diary, were "the greatest outrage history ever witnessed."

Anthony, 28, shows off a fashionable new outfit. Inspired by her elegant cousin Margaret, she had abandoned the Quakers' severe dress code a few years earlier.

T W O

Influences

Daniel Anthony was born in 1794 near Adams, Massachusetts, a small farming community in the western part of the state. He grew up deeply committed to the Quaker faith—and as an independent thinker. The Quaker church did not allow its members to "marry out of meeting" (marry a non-Quaker), but when Anthony fell in love with an attractive and high-spirited young Baptist woman, he courted her anyway.

Lucy Read had been raised by liberal parents who encouraged her to sing, wear pretty clothes, and attend dances and parties. Although their parents opposed the match, Anthony and Read were married in 1817. At that time, it was taken for granted that a wife would adopt her husband's religion and life-style. Because the Quaker faith forbade such worldly pleasures as singing, dancing, and stylish clothing, Lucy Read gave them all up when she became Mrs. Daniel Anthony.

During the next 16 years, Lucy Anthony bore 8 children, 6 of whom lived. The oldest was Guelma, born in 1818; next came Susan on February 15, 1820, then two more daughters and two sons. (Susan was named for her father's sister, Susannah Anthony Brownell; she never liked her middle name, Brownell, and soon shortened it to the initial *B*.) To support his growing family, Daniel Anthony built a small cotton mill. Both because cotton cloth enjoyed increasing popularity in the United States, and because Anthony was a good manager, the mill pros-

An 1854 daguerreotype shows Daniel Anthony at the age of 60. Daguerreotyping, an early form of photography, required subjects to hold poses a painfully long time.

A somberly garbed Lucy Read Anthony sits for a portrait in 1854. Once fond of dancing and pretty clothes, she changed her ways when she married Daniel Anthony.

pered and soon employed more than a dozen young women. Most of these millworkers, who came from nearby mountain towns, boarded with the Anthonys.

Running a household, raising six children, and cooking, sewing, washing, and ironing for both family and boarders kept Lucy Anthony's hands full. Once full of smiles and songs, she became withdrawn and silent, worn down by frequent pregnancies and endless toil. As an adult, Susan Anthony would say that her father probably

never realized how hard her mother had to work.

As soon as they were old enough, the Anthony children joined their mother in her daily labors, which included spinning, weaving, and carrying buckets of water to the kitchen from a nearby spring. Little Susan was also responsible for wiping the dishes, setting the table, and preparing food for the boarders' dinner pails.

Susan, Guelma, and Hannah, who was 18 months younger than Susan, were very close; when they were not doing their chores together, they could usually be found in the attic, playing endless games of make-believe. The sisters also loved to visit their grandmother Anthony. Susan long cherished happy memories of the raids she and her sisters made on their grandmother's tub of maple sugar, and of the sweet cider and crispy doughnuts Grandmother Anthony offered them.

In 1824, while Lucy Anthony awaited the birth of her fourth child, she sent Susan and Guelma to live at their grandmother's house. While she had them under her care, Grandmother Anthony decided to teach the little girls to read. Four-year-old Susan, already noted for her quick mind and eager curiosity, was delighted. "We just loved those books," she wrote later, "and we pored over them."

In 1826 a wealthy cotton manufacturer offered Daniel Anthony a partnership in his large cotton mill in Battenville, New York. Recognizing a good opportunity when he saw one, Anthony sold his mill, piled his wife and children into a horse-drawn wagon, and moved them to Battenville, a pleasant village about 40 miles from Adams.

At first, Susan was happy in Battenville's one-room schoolhouse, but she soon outgrew its resources. "I studied arithmetic and wanted to learn long division," she recalled later, but "the teacher didn't know enough to teach me." Even if he had, he might not have

troubled; few people of the time saw any reason for a female to "bother her head" with higher mathematics.

Unlike most religious sects, the Society of Friends (Quakers) recognized women as men's equals in many respects. Quaker women were allowed to speak at meeting, or church services, and they could vote on church-related matters. At home, sons were not regarded as superior to daughters, and wives had almost as much influence as husbands in making domestic decisions.

Even in this relatively liberal setting, Daniel Anthony's attitudes were unusual. By insisting on marrying the woman he loved, he had defied Quaker conventions, and when the time came to educate his daughters, he continued to follow his own convictions. Unsatisfied with the limitations of the local school, he added a wing to the handsome brick house he had built for

Susan B. Anthony, second of Daniel and Lucy Anthony's six surviving children, was born in this Adams, Massachusetts, house on February 15, 1820.

Often praised for her skill with a needle, 11-year-old Susan Anthony embroidered her family's names and birthdates on this sampler in 1831.

his family, hired a competent teacher, and started his own school.

Attending the new school along with the Anthony children were several local youngsters. One of them later wrote a letter to Susan Anthony. "The year I spent at your father's," she said, "was the happiest of my whole long life.... It had never been my fortune before to live in a household with an educated man at its head." Daniel Anthony, recalled the letter-writer, "seemed to have an eye for everything, his business, the school, and every good work."

Daniel Anthony's "good work" extended to the laborers he employed in his mill. He not only paid them higher wages than those earned by most factory workers, he took on the responsibility for educating them. He started an evening school that, recalled his daughter Susan, "was unpopular not to attend. Half the employees of the factory were there, learning to read and write or spell. Father would do the teaching himself.... He regarded his employees as his family and his duty to give them mental culture."

From her father, Susan Anthony acquired what would be a lifelong respect for education. Her attitude toward temperance, or abstinence from alcohol, was also shaped by his views. Because Daniel Anthony was appalled by the number of women and children abused by drunken husbands, he conducted a long-running campaign against the sale and use of liquor. Storekeepers of the era traditionally concluded their transactions by offering customers a drink of rum, but when Anthony added a general store to his cotton factory, he refused to serve liquor. Although other businessmen warned him that his store would fail if he did not "treat" his patrons, he stuck to his principles.

Local patrons grumbled at first about dealing with a "temperance" store, but Anthony sold high-quality merchandise at low prices, and his store prospered. Susan, who observed her father's actions with quiet admira-

Women workers wind thread onto spools in a 19th-century factory. Daniel Anthony allowed 12-year-old Susan to spend 2 weeks at similar labor in his cotton mill.

tion, would one day take her place as a leader of the women's crusade for temperance. She was also to become a leading abolitionist, again inspired by her father, a passionate opponent of slavery.

Although Daniel Anthony was considered "radical" by many of his neighbors, he was still a man limited by his times. When Susan, at age 11, noticed that one of her father's female mill-workers seemed to be more experienced than the factory overseer, she asked why the woman could not have the man's job. Her father, she recalled later, answered her with a surprised look. "It would never do," said the progressive Daniel Anthony, "to have a woman overseer in the mill."

Active and industrious, Susan filled her days with schoolwork, cooking, knitting, weaving, and fine needlework, a skill at which she excelled. She was fascinated by her father's mill and eager to learn more about its operation. Then, when she was 12 years old, her father announced that one of his "spoolers"—young women who wound thread on wooden cylinders—was ill and would be unable to work

A Quaker woman shyly models the unadorned clothing prescribed by her faith. Until her mid-20s, Susan Anthony also dressed in the "plain" style.

for 2 weeks. Susan and her sister Hannah immediately begged to take the sick worker's place, but their mother vetoed the idea. A mill, she said, was no place for a mill owner's daughters.

Daniel Anthony, who admired his girls' independent attitudes, wanted to grant their request. After listening to his calm arguments and to Susan's urgent pleas, Lucy Anthony reluctantly agreed to let one of the girls work. Her husband said they could draw straws for the job; the winner would work for two weeks, then share her wages with the loser. To her delight, Susan won. After proudly reporting to the factory for the next two weeks, she received $3. With her half of the money, she bought her mother six coffee cups, a reward for letting her work.

Continuing to encourage his daughters' independence, Daniel Anthony set up a plan of employment for them. When Guelma was 15, she spent the summer teaching the younger children in her father's school. In the fall, she went to live in a nearby town where she tutored the children of a Quaker family in return for room, board, and a salary of $1 per week. At 16, she taught in the district school and earned $1.50 per week. A year behind her sister, Susan followed the same path, trailed by Hannah a year after that.

Most of Daniel Anthony's neighbors criticized him for letting his daughters work for wages. As the children of a

Temperance advocates attend an outdoor rally in 1846. Concerned by the rapid spread of alcoholism, thousands of Americans joined the antiliquor movement.

prosperous businessman, they said, the Anthony girls should spend their time at home, helping their mother and practicing their embroidery. Guelma, Susan, and Hannah, however, were delighted with the chance to live as adults and earn their own money. When Guelma turned 17, her father sent her to boarding school in Philadelphia, headquarters of the Quaker religion. The following year, 17-year-old Susan joined her sister in that Pennsylvania city.

Philadelphia's Select Seminary for Females was operated by a sternly

religious Quaker named Deborah Moulson. The aim of her school, she wrote, was to educate young ladies "according to moral discipline in simplicity of speech, behavior, and apparel." Such training, she asserted, would induce her students "to depart from that kind of dress and address which leads the youthful mind so far from the path of propriety."

Daniel Anthony escorted Susan to her new school in November 1837. Philadelphia was less than 300 miles from Battenville, but the trip took almost a week. Father and daughter traveled to Albany in an open, horse-drawn cart, then boarded a steamboat for the trip down the Hudson River to New York City. From there, they took a ferry, a train, a canal boat, and a stage coach. "Before reaching [Philadelphia]," notes Katharine Anthony in her 1954 biography, *Susan B. Anthony*, Susan "experienced every variety of transport in common use at the time and arrived an enlightened traveler."

Susan was apprehensive about living so far from her family, and when her father left for Battenville, she was overcome by homesickness. "Oh, what pangs were felt, it seemed impossible for me to part with him," she wrote in her diary. "I could not speak to bid him farewell." Her gloomy feelings were not improved when she met

Taking matters—and axes—into their own hands, 19th-century temperance crusaders demolish barrels of liquor at a railroad depot in Kyana, Indiana.

headmistress Moulson, a formidable woman who believed that nothing in life was as important as "Morality, Humility, and Love of Virtue."

Everything Susan did, it seemed, earned Moulson's disapproval. According to her, Susan laughed too much and thought too little. She did not, said Moulson, even dot her *i*'s correctly! Bewildered by this barrage of criticism, Susan began to lose self-confidence. "I think so much of my resolutions to do better," she confided in her diary, "that even my dreams are filled with these desires." In another entry, she noted that Moulson had "reproved" her for displaying "levity and mirthfulness." Susan tried to understand the reasons for Moulson's reproofs, but, she wrote, "I do not consider myself as having committed any wilful offense. Perhaps I cannot see my own defects because my heart is hardened. O, may it become more and more refined until nothing shall remain but perfect purity."

Moulson's close watch on her pupils included censoring their mail. When a student wanted to write home, she had to compose her letter on a slate and give it to the headmistress. Moulson would revise it and return it to the student, who was then allowed to copy it carefully with a quill pen and mail it. In later years, Anthony would complain that all spontaneity in her writing style had perished under Moulson's strict hand. "Whenever I take my pen

in hand," she said, "I seem to be mounted on stilts."

On February 15, Susan Anthony wrote in her diary, "This day I call myself 18. It seems impossible that I can be so old, and even at this age I find myself possessed of no more knowledge than I ought to have had at 12." Soon afterward, she sent a letter to a friend without first submitting it to Moulson. A few days later, she was summoned to the headmistress's office. She went, as she put it in her diary, "with cheerfulness," but her heart sank when she saw Moulson at her desk, the "illegal" letter clutched in her hand. After she had received a blistering lecture on her wrongdoing, Anthony wrote sadly, "Little did I think when I was writing that letter that I was committing such an enormous crime."

Life at the seminary did have occasional bright spots. Anthony enjoyed sleigh riding with other students and going on field trips to Philadelphia's Academy of Arts and Sciences. She also liked her science courses. In a letter to her parents, she reported on having "the pleasure of viewing the dust from the wings of a butterfly" through a microscope. "Each minute particle," she said excitedly, "appeared as large as a common fly." And at Moulson's school, Anthony got to know a student teacher, Lydia Mott, who would become her lifelong close friend and associate.

"The Drunkard's Pilgrimage," a typically dramatic temperance poster, illustrates the *"horrible fate"* that awaits a young man who so much as tastes wine.

In 1838, the United States was swept by a severe financial depression, and Susan Anthony's school days ended abruptly. She learned that her father's business had been ruined, his fortune wiped out. She was not distressed to learn she had to leave the seminary, but the loss of the family home grieved her deeply. "O can I ever forget that loved residence in Battenville," she wrote in her diary. "No more to call it home seems impossible."

Soon after she returned to Battenville, Anthony was offered a teaching position in a neighboring town. She had enjoyed working when it was voluntary, but now that it was necessary, it seemed less appealing. In May 1838, she wrote in her diary, "I again left my home to mingle with strangers, which seems to be my sad lot. Separation was rendered more trying on account of the embarrassing condition of our business affairs."

The following spring, the Anthonys' home and its contents were sold at public auction in order to pay Daniel Anthony's business debts. Not only the house, but everything the family owned, from furniture and books to clothing and even eyeglasses was offered for sale. Susan Anthony, who had been saving her small teacher's salary over the year, was able to buy back some of her parents' most treasured possessions. With wistful pride, she noted in her diary, "I purchased things to the amount of 11 dollars."

Lucy Anthony was comforted by her daughter's action. Her distress was also eased when her brother bought and returned to her some of the furniture and silver she had received as wedding gifts. Because a married woman could legally own nothing, everything that had "belonged" to Lucy Anthony was the property of her husband and could be used to satisfy his debts. This injustice burned itself into Susan Anthony's brain.

After the sale, the Anthonys moved to the nearby village of Hardscrabble, later called Center Falls. Their new house, a former tavern, was far less elegant than the large brick home they had left behind, but their spirits remained high. Sympathetic friends paid frequent visits, and Susan and her sisters were showered with invitations to quilting parties, buggy rides, and picnics. Many years later, in fact, Lucy Anthony called the period after her husband's bankruptcy the happiest of her life.

After the move, Susan Anthony worked harder than ever around the house. Her diary from these days contains such entries as: "Did a large washing today"; "Spent today at the spinning wheel"; "Baked 21 loaves of bread"; "Have been weaving for several days past; yesterday and today wove 3 yards."

Although she was useful at home, Anthony decided she could help her family more by getting a salaried job. In the spring of 1840, she went to teach at a boarding school in New Rochelle,

Ridiculing the idea of female independence, an 1884 cartoon shows women in such "unthinkable" jobs as letter carrier, firefighter, soldier, and police officer.

American Anti-Slavery Almanac for 1840.

The seven cuts following, are selected from thirteen, which may be found in the Anti-Slavery Almanac for 1840. They represent well-authenticated facts, and illustrate in various ways, the cruelties daily inflicted upon three millions of native born Americans, by their fellow-countrymen! A brief explanation follows each cut.

The peculiar "Domestic Institutions of our Southern brethren."

Selling a Mother from her Child.

Mothers with young Children at work in the field.

A Woman chained to a Girl, and a Man in irons at work in the field.

"They can't take care of themselves"; explained in an interesting article.

A Slave drowned.

Servility of the Northern States in arresting and returning fugitive Slaves.

Printed in an 1840 antislavery publication, these drawings were said to illustrate "the cruelties daily inflicted upon 3 millions of native-born Americans."

not far from New York City. There, she heard much talk about the abolition of slavery. Like her father, she considered slavery an unmitigated evil, and she approved of the attitudes expressed by the people of New Rochelle. She soon realized, however, that they did not always practice what they preached.

With disgust, she recorded her impressions of a local Quaker service she attended. "The Friends raised quite a fuss about a colored man sitting in the meeting-house, and some left on account of it. The man was . . . very polite, but still the pretended meek followers of Christ could not worship their God and have this sable [black] companion with them. What a lack of Christianity is this!"

Anthony also noted that three "educated and refined" young black women visiting the Quaker meeting were "not allowed to sit even on the back seat. One long-faced elder dusted off a seat in the gallery [balcony] and told them to sit there." After this, Anthony made a point of being gracious to the black visitors. In a letter to a friend, she said, "I have had the unspeakable satisfaction of . . . drinking tea with them. They are indeed fine *ladies*. To show this kind of people respect in this heathen land affords me a double pleasure."

In September 1840, Anthony returned to Center Falls to attend her sister Guelma's wedding. In order to remain close to home, she took a job teaching in the local district school, replacing a male teacher who had been dismissed for inefficiency. He had been paid $10 per week, but her salary—because she was a woman—was $2.50.

Perhaps more distressing, her pupils baited and taunted their new teacher. She tried to reason with the group's ringleader, but without success. One day, however, the tall, rebellious pupil pushed her too far. She cut a stick, took him behind the school, and gave him a memorable beating. He gave her no more trouble.

As she moved from place to place over the next few years, working either as a governess or teacher, Anthony received several proposals of marriage. Most women of the time dreaded the thought of remaining single after the age of 20, but Anthony was unusually independent. She turned down all of her suitors.

In her diary, Anthony recorded dreams about getting married, but she also expressed unflattering opinions about those who actually asked for her hand. She described one, for example, as a "real soft-headed old bachelor." Reacting to the marriage of a friend, she wrote, "Tis passing strange that a girl possessed of common sense should be willing to marry a lunatic— but so it is."

Anthony was increasingly disturbed, too, about men's patronizing attitudes toward women. She felt this tension even with Aaron McLean, Guelma's husband and Susan's old and dear friend. One day, as Anthony served him a plate of her celebrated cream biscuits, she proudly told him she was learning algebra. "I'd rather see a woman make biscuits like these than solve the knottiest problem in algebra," he said. "There is no reason," she shot back, "why she should not be able to do both."

After his financial downfall, Daniel Anthony tried logging, innkeeping, and working as a millhand, but none provided a satisfactory living. In 1845, he decided to move again, this time to Rochester, New York. With help from his wife's brother, he bought a farm, packed up his household, and headed west on the Erie Canal. Traveling with Anthony and his wife were their three younger children, Susan, Mary, and Merritt. In Rochester, the Anthonys received a warm welcome from their Quaker neighbors, many of whom shared Daniel and Susan Anthony's strong feelings about the abolition and temperance movements.

Listening to the antislavery activists who gathered at her family's farm, Susan Anthony heard with mounting horror stories about the abuse of black people on the plantations of the South. She was heartened to learn about the Underground Railroad, an informal network of abolitionists who secretly helped guide fugitive slaves to safety in the North and Canada. She and her father often talked long into the night, debating the serious issues that divided pro- and antislavery factions and that would one day divide the nation.

When Susan Anthony was 26 years old, her uncle, Joshua Read, arranged

Impassive white customers look on as a slave auctioneer takes bids on a black woman and her daughter—available for sale together or separately.

for her appointment as headmistress of the "female department" at Canajoharie Academy, a prestigious school in upstate New York. She taught there from 1846 to 1849, boarding with Joshua Read's married daughter, Margaret Caldwell. Exposed for the first time to life in a non-Quaker household, Anthony shed some of her Quaker ways. She had always worn the somber, traditional costume of Quaker women; now, following the example of her cousin Margaret, she began to wear colorful, stylish clothes. In a letter to her family, she excitedly described a recent purchase: "I have a new pearl straw gypsy hat, trimmed in white ribbon with a fringe on one edge and a pink satin stripe on the other, with a few white roses and green leaves for inside trimming."

Under Margaret Caldwell's influence, Anthony even began to enjoy such "worldly" pastimes as theatergoing. She wrote to her brother Daniel about one invitation she had received. "I believe I will accept," she said, "as I have never attended a circus. I might see something to amuse my young mind."

Already an experienced and competent teacher, Anthony quickly acquired a glowing reputation as a headmistress. Schools of the period conducted annual "public examinations" in which pupils demonstrated their learning for parents and school board members. Anthony's first such examination was a resounding success, resulting in a shower of compliments for the "schoolmarm." One resident probably spoke for many when he pronounced Anthony "the smartest woman who ever came to Canajoharie."

Anthony's sisters Guelma and Hannah, however, were not so sure about her "smartness." Puzzled by her refusal to marry, they often teased her about being "an old maid." She teased them back, pointing out that as an employed, single woman, she could afford to buy elegant dresses and other luxuries. Writing to her mother about her newly wed sister, Hannah, she said, "I suppose she feels rather sad that she is married and can no longer have nice clothes."

As unenthusiastic as ever about her suitors, Anthony turned down two marriage proposals during her stay in Canajoharie. She was particularly critical of men who drank liquor. After one party, she wrote in her diary, "I certainly shall not attend another dance unless I can have a total abstinence man to accompany me, and not one whose highest delight is to make a fool of himself." And to her sister Mary, she wrote indignantly, "I can assure you not so much that I was at a dance as that I was a witness to brandy-sipping."

Anthony's opinion of men was not raised by the behavior of her cousin Margaret's husband. When Margaret lay desperately ill after the birth of her fourth child, her husband once complained of a headache. Anthony wrote her mother that, when the sick woman said she had one, too, her husband replied, "Oh, mine is the real headache, genuine pain, yours is a sort of natural consequence." A few weeks later, Margaret Caldwell was dead. Anthony would never forget this display of callousness.

She had now reached a crossroads in her life. At the age of 29, she had risen to the top of her profession, but the life of a "schoolmarm," even one who was highly regarded, offered little

At an Indiana stop on the Underground Railroad, a white farm woman and her husband offer shelter to fugitive slaves on their way to freedom in Canada.

challenge. Still, options for women, even for a woman with Anthony's intelligence, idealism, and drive, remained limited in the mid-19th century. Deeply grieved by her cousin's death, unsure where her life was going, Anthony decided to return to her family in Rochester. There, within a short period of time, one of the most remarkable careers in the history of American women would begin to take shape.

The shocking "bloomer costume," seen here in an 1851 magazine illustration, inspired either furious indignation or derisive laughter from most observers.

THREE

Friends and Causes

When Susan Anthony came home to Rochester in 1849, she found her family and friends preoccupied with the subject of slavery. After Texas had been admitted to the Union as a slave state in 1845, the nation had split into two camps. One asserted that each new state had the right to make its own decision about slavery; the other insisted that no more slavery-permitting territories should be allowed to enter the Union.

Most members of the antislavery movement believed in limiting the expansion of slavery rather than eliminating it altogether. The movement, however, included a splinter group whose goal was immediate freedom for all slaves. Among this abolitionist minority was Susan Anthony's father, Daniel. Along with a number of other Quakers, he had left the conservative Society of Friends and joined the Unitarian Church, which supported immediate emancipation.

The Anthony farm had become the informal center of activity for abolitionists in the area. Each Sunday, a crowd of men and women, all passionately dedicated to the eradication of slavery, gathered around the Anthony dinner table to discuss ways to accomplish their goal. Among the most frequent guests was Daniel Anthony's good friend, Frederick Douglass, a former slave who had become one of the nation's most effective voices for abolition. Dividing her time between serving food and listening to her father's visitors, Susan Anthony heard Douglass and other activists cautiously discussing their work in helping runaway slaves find freedom. Like her father, she became an uncompromising abo-

Former slave Frederick Douglass fought for black emancipation, but he opposed the uncompromising policies of William Lloyd Garrison and other militant abolitionists.

litionist, supporting immediate emancipation and scorning those who advised patience and moderation.

She wholeheartedly adopted the "radical" abolitionists' battle cry, words she would follow for the rest of her life: "Shall I tell a man whose house is on fire to give a moderate alarm; tell him moderately to rescue his wife from the hands of a ravisher; tell the mother gradually to extricate her babe from the fire into which it has fallen? . . . I am in earnest—I will not equivocate—I will not excuse—I will not retreat a single inch—and I will be heard!"

Another major issue of the day was temperance. Ever since the early days of the republic, liquor had been both plentiful and cheap in the United States. Its manufacture and sale were virtually unregulated, and its use, even to excess, was condoned at all levels of society. Many people felt that drunkenness had become a serious problem, particularly for the wives of alcohol abusers. Such women were powerless to help themselves: Their assets and earnings, even their children, belonged to their husbands, who could do with them as they pleased. Drunken husbands could batter their wives with impunity: Wife-beating was not a crime, and alcoholism was not recognized as grounds for divorce. When divorces were granted, it was assumed that fathers, abusive or not, would keep the children.

The American temperance movement, which aimed at controlling or eliminating the consumption of alcohol, began to gain momentum in the 1830s. By 1849, it was a well-organized and increasingly powerful political force, with local reform societies operating across the land. Among the most active of these societies was a group known as the Sons of Temperance.

Although women were the main victims of alcohol abuse, they were barred

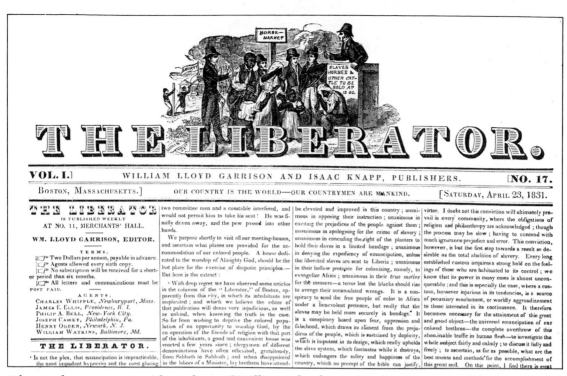

THE LIBERATOR.

VOL. I.]   WILLIAM LLOYD GARRISON AND ISAAC KNAPP, PUBLISHERS.   [NO. 17.

BOSTON, MASSACHUSETTS.]   OUR COUNTRY IS THE WORLD—OUR COUNTRYMEN ARE MANKIND.   [SATURDAY, APRIL 23, 1831.

The Anthonys were avid readers of William Lloyd Garrison's newspaper, The Liberator, *which demanded the "TOTAL and IMMEDIATE abolition" of slavery.*

from any active role in the Sons of Temperance or other reform organizations. They were permitted to join auxiliary groups called Daughters of Temperance but could not vote or even speak at the men's meetings. Women, said the male reformers, belonged in the home, not in public life. Nevertheless, women flocked to the temperance movement. For Susan B. Anthony, already committed to the cause and eager for a challenge, joining the Daughters of Temperance was a natural step.

It was at an 1849 women's temperance meeting in Canajoharie that Anthony made her first public speech. Hoping to interest local people in its work, the Daughters invited 200 men and women to a picnic supper; after the meal, Anthony rose nervously and began to read the words she had carefully written for the occasion.

"We do not assume that females possess unbounded power in abolishing the evil customs of the day," she said, "but we do believe that were they . . . to discontinue the use of wine and brandy at both their public and private parties, not one of the opposite sex . . . would so insult them as to come into their presence after having quaffed of that foul destroyer of all true delicacy and refinement." Warming to her subject, she raised her voice and said, "Ladies! There is no neutral position

An alcoholic leads his long-suffering wife and children to disgrace in "The Bad Husband," a sentimental and very popular temperance-movement poster.

for us to assume. . . . Permit me once more to beg of you to lend your aid to this great cause, the cause of God and all mankind!"

Her speech was a success, and Anthony became increasingly active in the temperance movement. Discovering—somewhat to her own surprise—that she had a real gift for leadership, she began to organize fairs and suppers for the Rochester chapter of the Daughters of Temperance, raising much-needed money for the group's work. Her fellow crusaders, impressed by her abilities, elected her to represent them at a major temperance convention to be held in Albany, New York, in early 1852. It was to be a turning point in her life.

The convention was sponsored by the Sons of Temperance, which had invited the Daughters of Temperance to send delegates. Far from the men's minds, however, was the idea of letting the women participate in the proceedings. Thus, when Susan Anthony rose to make a point, a buzz of male outrage filled the hall. Shocked, the chairman demanded silence.

"The sisters," he thundered, "were not invited here to speak, but to listen and learn." A furious Anthony swept from the room, followed by a handful of other women. Those who remained joined the men in their disapproval of these "unladylike" delegates; they were, said one stern matriarch, nothing but "bold, meddlesome disturbers."

Although the word *bold* had not been used as a compliment, it suited Anthony well. Dismayed but not discouraged by her treatment by the Sons of Temperance, she decided to hold her own meeting for women that very night. After renting a basement room in a nearby church, she talked with her friend Thurlow Weed, editor of the Albany *Evening Journal*. The sympathetic Weed ran a story in his evening edition, describing Anthony's experience at the convention and announcing the time and location of her meeting.

Not many people braved the cold, snowy night to attend the meeting. The badly lit basement room grew even dimmer when the stovepipe collapsed, sending out a cloud of smoke in the middle of Anthony's speech. Nevertheless, those who attended were fired with enthusiasm for the creation of a role for women in the temperance movement. By the end of the evening, the group had a firm plan: It would sponsor a statewide women's temperance convention under the direction of Susan Anthony.

After settling on the following April as the time for the rally, Anthony wrote to women's associations across New York State, asking each to send delegates. Assisting and encouraging her was a new friend: Elizabeth Cady Stanton, an ardent supporter of another new movement as well. Stanton's cause was women's rights.

American society had traditionally considered women mentally inferior to men, a view solidly endorsed by organized religion. Clergymen cited the Bible to prove that women's intellectual abilities were of a lower order and that women were therefore unsuited to any roles but those of wives and mothers. Women were barred from institutions of higher learning and excluded from professions outside a few specified and low-paid areas, such as teaching and millwork. Women, of course, were also denied the right to vote—a right that would have given them some power to change their lives. For generations, such restrictions, based on English law and imported to the United States, had stood unchallenged.

This unquestioning acceptance of the notion of female inferiority had started to erode in 1848, when Elizabeth Cady Stanton and Lucretia Mott (an aunt of Lydia Mott, Susan Anthony's schoolmate) organized a convention in Seneca Falls, New York. This meeting, called "to discuss the social, civil, and religious rights of women," was to mark the start of the American women's rights movement.

The Sons of Temperance admitted only "brothers," a shortsighted policy that deprived the organization of a valuable potential asset: American women.

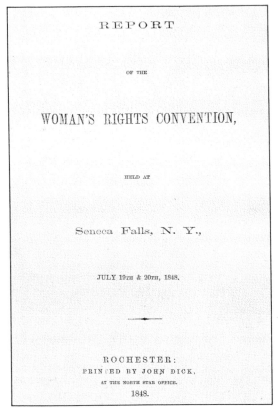

REPORT

OF THE

WOMAN'S RIGHTS CONVENTION,

HELD AT

Seneca Falls, N. Y.,

JULY 19TH & 20TH, 1848.

ROCHESTER:
PRINTED BY JOHN DICK,
AT THE NORTH STAR OFFICE.
1848.

The 1848 Woman's Rights Convention report contained Stanton's radical "Declaration of Rights and Sentiments," which included a demand for woman suffrage.

To present the case for women, Stanton wrote a manifesto, the "Declaration of Rights and Sentiments," based on the American Declaration of Independence. Its opening words, unsurprising today, were revolutionary in 1848: "We hold these truths to be self-evident: that all men and women are created equal."

The document went on to present a series of resolutions that called for giving women the right to own property, to speak freely, to sue for divorce, and to enter educational and professional fields on an equal footing with men. Most of the 300 women attending the convention supported these resolutions, but many were shocked by the last demand on Stanton's list: that women be given the right to vote. Despite widespread opposition to this "ultraradical" idea, Stanton insisted on leaving it in the declaration, and the convention finally approved it by a narrow margin.

Newspapers and clergymen reacted to the Seneca Falls meeting with outrage. Called "The Hen Convention," it was denounced as a conspiracy against the home, against the purity of American women, against heaven itself. Its participants, said critics, were nothing but a collection of "cranks," "hermaphrodites," and "atheists."

When Anthony first read about the Seneca Falls Convention, she was not impressed. She was astonished to discover that her parents and many of their Quaker friends had not only approved of the Declaration of Rights and Sentiments, but had signed copies of it. When Daniel Anthony told his daughter he supported the idea of woman suffrage, she laughed. "I think," she said, "you are getting a good deal ahead of the times."

Nonetheless, her family talked so much about the new movement for women's rights, and about the brilliant

Addressing the 1848 convention at Seneca Falls, New York, Elizabeth Cady Stanton helps launch the American women's rights movement.

Elizabeth Cady Stanton, that Anthony's interest was piqued. She decided she would like to meet this unusual woman and learn more about the cause to which she was so passionately dedicated. In 1851, she got her chance.

Visiting Seneca Falls to attend a lecture by the famous abolitionist William Lloyd Garrison, Anthony stayed with her friend Amelia Bloomer. Bloomer, who edited the *Lily*, a small temperance newspaper, had popularized a revolutionary new women's clothing style: wide trousers worn under a knee-length skirt. Although she had not invented the fashion, she had publicized it in her newspaper, and the outfit had become known as the "bloomer costume," later shortened to "bloomers."

As Anthony and Bloomer walked home from Garrison's lecture, they met

Stanton, a Seneca Falls resident and friend of Bloomer's. Years later, Stanton recalled her introduction to Anthony, which started a lifelong friendship, and which would become one of the motivating forces behind the woman-suffrage movement in the United States. "There she stood with her good, earnest face and genial smile, dressed in gray," said Stanton, who added that she saw her new acquaintance as "the perfection of neatness and sobriety."

The two women were superficially most unlike each other. At 31, Anthony was tall, slim, reserved, and single. Stanton, 36, was short, plump, and outgoing, the happily married mother of 3 boys. Nevertheless, they felt an immediate kinship. Wrote Stanton later, "I liked her thoroughly from the beginning." Stanton would introduce Anthony to other women's-rights ad-

Elizabeth Cady Stanton embraces two of her six children. A loving mother, Stanton divided her time between her family and her crusade for women's rights.

vocates, including Horace Greeley, the influential editor of the reform newspaper the New York *Tribune*, and Lucy Stone, who would herself become a major figure in the history of the women's movement.

Anthony found her new female acquaintances fascinating, but she was rather startled by their adoption of the scandalous bloomer costume. Conventional female clothes of the period consisted of tight corsets, long, awkward petticoats, and stiff, hooped skirts, all of which inhibited movement and made breathing difficult. In contrast, bloomers gave women freedom and comfort, a notion that most men—

and many women—found threatening. The wearing of bloomers, in fact, provoked louder protests than any other feminist practice.

Although the costume covered the legs, it revealed that its wearer *had* legs, something no "lady" would admit. Clergymen called bloomers "devilish," and the press mocked "those women dressed like men." Women who wore bloomers were taunted unmercifully when they walked down the street. Even Stanton's husband, usually supportive of her crusade for women's rights, laughed at his wife's costume. Her father asked her to abandon it. "No woman of good sense and delicacy," he said, "would make such a guy of herself." The costume, however, was an enormously important symbol of freedom to its wearers. Stanton wrote an article defending it.

"For us commonplace, everyday, working characters," she said, "who wash and iron, bake and brew, carry water and fat babies upstairs and down, bring potatoes, apples, and pans of milk from the cellar, run our own errands through mud or snow; shovel paths and work in the garden, why 'the drapery' [long skirts] is too much—one might as well work with a ball and chain."

Although initially shocked by the sight of women in bloomers, Anthony grew to admire Stanton and Stone deeply, and a year after she met them, she donned the revolutionary outfit herself. Writing to Stone in 1852, she said, "Well, at last I am in short skirt and trousers." Her appearance in bloomers gave hostile reporters a field day. One of them reported that her "ungainly form rigged out in the bloomer costume [provoked] laughter and ridicule."

Convinced that wearing bloomers "involves a principle of freedom," Elizabeth Stanton endured the abuse of press and public for three years. At last, however, she decided that there were more important issues than costume. "We put it on for greater freedom," she said in an 1854 letter to Anthony, "but what is physical freedom compared with mental bondage?" Stanton let down her hems, as did Stone.

Anthony stuck to her guns for another year, but finally she, too, relented, reasoning that her effectiveness as a speaker was diminished by her audiences' curiosity about her attire. In a letter to Stanton, she said, "To be successful, a person must attempt only one reform, and I shall always fight to keep women's rights free from every other issue." Like Stanton, she had decided that the defiant wearing of

Trousered women were a great joke in the 1800s. "Don't stand there with your hands in your pockets," says this mother. "You don't know how ungentlemanly it looks!"

unconventional clothing put the cart before the horse. Comfortable clothing would not free women. To be truly comfortable, women would have to be free.

By the time she was 32, Anthony had become an expert organizer and the firm friend of Elizabeth Stanton. Together, the two women would make history.

FOUR

A Purse of Her Own

Susan B. Anthony and Elizabeth Cady Stanton would become one of the most effective teams in American political history. Their first joint undertaking, however, ended in failure. It was aimed at strengthening the position of women in the temperance movement.

After she stormed out of the Sons of Temperance convention in January 1852, Anthony and her supporters voted to hold a statewide temperance meeting for women. Stanton reacted to the news with an enthusiastic letter to Anthony. "I will gladly do all in my power to help you," she wrote. More experienced at public speaking than her younger friend, Stanton offered to write a speech for her. She also gave her some tips about lecturing: "Dress loosely, take a great deal of exercise, be particular about your diet and sleep enough. . . . In your meetings, if attacked, be cool and good-natured, for if you are simple and truth-loving no sophistry [sly argument] can confound you."

Buoyed by Stanton's faith that she would become "an admirable speaker" and eager to involve more women in the temperance movement, Anthony spent the months before the convention in a whirlwind of activity. She wrote hundreds of letters asking for financial and moral support, traveled from town to town explaining the project to women, hired a convention hall in Rochester, invited prominent people to speak, and arranged for posters and newspaper advertisements.

Her hard work paid off. When the convention opened in April 1852, more than 500 women packed the hall. Addressing her listeners in a clear, strong

This 1850 lithograph implies equality between Daughters and Sons of Temperance, but in reality, the movement's men ignored women. Their attitude infuriated Anthony.

voice, Anthony said all women should work "for the protection of their interests and of society at large, too long invaded and destroyed by legalized intemperance." The crowd applauded as one speaker after another confirmed the need for women's involvement in the temperance movement.

As Anthony had planned, the group voted to establish the Women's State Temperance Society and to install Stanton as its first president. Anthony was named secretary, assigned to do everything "necessary to promote the purposes for which our society has been organized."

This endeavor in many ways typified the partnership of Anthony and Stanton throughout the next 50 years. Fiery, fearless, and brilliant, Stanton always pursued her ideas to their limit. Even at the first convention of the Women's State Temperance Society, she shocked her audience with the radical demand that women be given the right to divorce their husbands on the grounds of drunkenness. Many people considered marriage sacred, believing that nothing—not even a husband's abusiveness—justified divorce. These conservatives also felt Stanton's calls for women's rights diverted attention from the issue of temperance. But Stanton believed that all such issues were linked to the oppression of women.

Stanton's idealism was a perfect complement to Anthony's practical skills as a tactician—skills that would one day earn her a reputation as "the Napoleon of the women's rights movement." Stanton inspired Anthony with ideas and possibilities. But it was Anthony who would travel relentlessly across the country, mobilizing support for women's rights and recruiting thousands of supporters to the cause. Said Henry Stanton to his wife some years later: "You stir up Susan and she stirs up the world."

The women established this pattern of working together early in their rela-

Male saloon patrons bow their heads as women temperance workers pray for them. "Prayer raids," although well intentioned, rarely accomplished their goals.

tionship. Because Anthony had greater mobility than Stanton, who had a growing family, the two usually met in Seneca Falls. Together they mapped out strategy, worked on correspondence, and planned lectures. Stanton composed most of the speeches, and Anthony delivered them.

In one tongue-in-cheek letter to her colleague, Anthony urged her to write an important speech quickly. "For the love of me and for the saving of the reputation of womankind," she wrote, "I beg you with one baby on your knee and another at your feet and four boys whistling [and] buzzing . . . set yourself about the work." Repeating her plea, Anthony asked her friend to "load my gun, leaving me only to pull the trigger and let fly the powder and ball."

In her *Reminiscences*, Stanton wrote about herself and Anthony. "We never met without issuing a pronunciamento [proclamation] on some question," she said. "[Anthony] supplied facts and statistics, I the philosophy and rhetoric, and together, we have made arguments that have stood unshaken by the storms of nearly 50 long years."

To allow Stanton time to write, Anthony often took over her household chores. Stanton's daughter, Harriot, later wrote, "They had such a good time. There was so much happiness in their union. Aunt Susan used to take

Most 19th-century newspapers recognized drunkenness as a major problem. This cartoon is captioned, "No wonder the wives of these men have joined the praying band."

care of us children while mother wrote a speech." And one of Stanton's sons recalled, "Little did we think, in our younger days, when we beheld . . . mother and Susan scratching away at speeches, petitions, resolutions, what big guns they were to be."

After the Women's State Temperance Society had been established, Anthony traveled all over New York State, raising money, recruiting members, and organizing new chapters. Within a year, more than 1,000 women and men had joined the society. When the Sons of Temperance, which now called itself the Men's State Temperance Society, scheduled a convention in Syracuse, it invited the women's group to send delegates. Anthony and Bloomer were chosen to represent their colleagues.

The women had assumed that the men's invitation signaled a new willingness to work with them. They were wrong. The majority of the delegates in Syracuse were clergymen, traditionally the strongest opponents of rights for women. When Anthony and Bloomer arrived at the convention, they learned that its participants had changed their minds about the presence of women: They were no longer welcome. Refusing to leave, they took their places in the hall. Pandemonium followed.

One after another, black-garbed ministers rose to shout that they would not sit with "those females." They were not females, cried one delegate, but "a hybrid species, half man and half woman, belonging to neither sex." Such creatures, said another man, had no business disrupting a temperance meeting by preaching their "dreadful doctrines of women's rights, divorce, and atheism." Anthony managed to announce that she had brought temperance petitions signed by more than 100,000 women, but it did no good. Within minutes, amid a torrent of screamed insults, she and Bloomer were forcibly ejected from the hall.

Anthony was beginning to think Stanton might be right in her assertion that women would have to gain legal rights before anybody would listen to their views. After Syracuse, her temperance speeches included an appeal for laws that would permit the wives of drunkards to obtain divorces. This approach—which one newspaper labeled an "attempt to ride the woman's rights theory into respectability on the back of Temperance"—drew even more abuse.

Reporting on one of her lectures, the Utica *Evening Standard* said that Anthony had "announced quite confidently that wives don't . . . love their husbands if they are dissipated [drink to excess]. Everyday observation proves the utter falsity of this statement." The attacks on Anthony's philosophy often became brutally direct. Calling her "personally repulsive," the Utica *Evening Telegraph* said "she seems to be laboring under feelings of strong hatred towards . . . men, the effect, we presume, of jealousy and neglect."

Still another newspaper observed, "With a degree of impiety [ungodliness] which was both startling and disgusting, this shrewish *maiden* counseled the numerous wives and mothers present to separate from their husbands whenever they became intemperate, *and particularly not to allow the said husbands to add another child to the family.* . . . Think of such advice given in public by one who claims to be a *maiden* lady!"

Anthony's stormy involvement with the temperance movement came to an end in 1853. Although the Women's State Temperance Society permitted only women to be officers, it allowed men to join and to speak at meetings. By the organization's second year, its feminist members were outnumbered by conservative men and their female supporters. Under pressure from this group, President Stanton agreed to allow men to run for office. She hoped this move would increase harmony within the society, but it had the opposite effect.

Immediately voting to change the group's name to The People's League,

Needing no words to make its point, a temperance poster shows a child sacrificed on the altar of "profit," a clear reference to the liquor industry.

the male-led group ousted Stanton from the presidency. They reelected Anthony as secretary, but she refused to serve; she and Stanton resigned from the organization they had created. Anthony's distress over this turn of events was allayed by her friend. "We have," said Stanton serenely, "other and bigger fish to fry."

The People's League disintegrated soon after the two women departed. Not until 20 years later, when the Women's Christian Temperance Union was founded, would women again play an active role in the temperance movement. After the collapse of the original society, Stanton repeated her contention that women could accomplish little until their fundamental rights had been secured. She asked Anthony, "Do you see, at last?" Anthony replied, "At last, I see."

Anthony and Stanton's next major campaign directly addressed a women's-rights issue. They set out to win property rights for married women in New York State. Like many other feminists, they regarded the current law, which decreed that the possessions and earnings of married women belonged to their husbands, as a major injustice.

Anthony had decided to concentrate on this issue after she attended an 1843 women's-rights convention in Cleveland, Ohio. On her way home, she stopped to visit some of the local chapters of the State Temperance Society she had founded earlier. Not one

was still in operation. They had failed for lack of financial support, their female members having no money of their own. The situation infuriated her.

In her journal, she wrote, "I never took in so fully the grand idea of [financial] independence. Woman must have a purse of her own, and how can this be, so long as the law denies to the wife all right to both the individual and joint earnings? There is no true freedom for woman without the possession of equal property rights, and these can be obtained only through legislation."

Obtaining such legislation from Albany's all-male lawmakers would be a formidable task. Stanton and Anthony divided up the work: Stanton would write and deliver a speech to a joint meeting of the state senate and assembly, and Anthony would circulate petitions supporting revised property laws. Anthony rounded up 60 volunteers, each responsible for collecting signatures in one part of the state. Trudging from house to house during the harsh winter of 1853–54, Anthony's workers found some support for their mission, but more often than not, they found doors slammed in their faces. Nevertheless, the determined army of volunteers obtained 6,000 signatures, and Anthony and Stanton felt prepared to challenge the state legislators.

Stanton, an eloquent speaker, outdid herself, delivering a moving and powerful address. Anthony spoke, too, ex-

Carry Nation, an antisaloon crusader famed for her direct approach, surveys the havoc she has wrought in a Kansas barroom. Anthony's methods were more moderate.

plaining the proposed new laws to a special committee of the legislature. Both women were heard in respectful silence, but when they finished, politicians from both parties rose to denounce their mission.

In a typical response, one man asked if he and his colleagues were expected "to give the least countenance to claims so preposterous, disgraceful, and criminal as are embodied in this address." Could they, he asked, "put the stamp of truth upon the libel ... that men and women ... are equal?" Then, getting to the heart of his argument, he said, "We *know* that God created man as the representative of the race; that after his creation the Creator took from his side the material for woman's creation; and that by the institution of matrimony, woman was restored to the side of man, and that they became one flesh and one being, he being the head."

The 1854 legislative session produced no new laws dealing with women's property rights. Anthony and Stanton were not surprised, but neither were they discouraged. Anthony told the legislators that she would appear before them every year until the laws were changed. And she was

Amelia Bloomer edited a newspaper, campaigned for temperance, and helped lead the women's rights movement, but she was best known for the costume named after her.

more keenly the degradation of my sex. To think that all in me of which my father would have felt a proper pride had I been a man is deeply mortifying to him because I am a woman. . . . Sometimes, Susan, I struggle in deep waters."

Stanton's problems—her father's disapproval and the demands of her husband and family—matched those of many women's-rights advocates. Anthony's experience was very different. Her father not only encouraged her reform activities but gave her financial support. Moreover, her life was free from domestic constraints. Still, at this time and later, she sometimes struggled with feelings of abandonment and loneliness.

She felt that the family commitments of Stanton and other women's-movement colleagues made them less intense about causes and friendships. In a letter to Stanton she wrote, "Those of you who have the *talent* to do honor to poor—oh! how poor—womanhood, have all given yourself over to baby-making and left poor brainless me to battle alone."

For the time being, she did battle alone. To advertise her lectures, she sent handbills to small towns all over the state, asking local sheriffs and post-masters to display them before she arrived. Then, packing her bag with campaign literature and petitions, she boarded the first of the many trains she would ride during the bitterly cold

gratified to receive loving words of support from her friend Lucy Stone. "God bless you, Susan dear, for the brave heart that will work on even in the midst of discouragement," she wrote. "The example of positive action is what we need."

The following fall, Anthony decided to visit every one of New York State's 60 counties, gathering a new sheaf of petitions for the Albany lawmakers. Stanton wanted to join her, but family responsibilities kept her at home. "I wish I were as free as you, and I would stump the state in a twinkling. But I am not, and what is more, I passed through a terrible scourging when last at my father's," she wrote. "I never felt

Leaving her husband in the kitchen, a bowler-hatted woman strides out to vote. Woman suffrage, warned its opponents, would make such scenes commonplace.

winter of 1855. Sleeping in country inns or chilly farmhouses, traveling sometimes by rail, sometimes by stage-coach or horse-drawn sleigh, she made her way through dozens of villages, towns, and cities. At each stop, she rented a hall where she lectured, answered questions, and distributed petitions.

Her commitment to married women's property rights was reaffirmed by some of her petition-gathering experi-

ences. In one village, she and a woman friend stayed at a tavern where, she reported in a letter to her family, "the landlady was not yet 20 and had a baby, 15 months old. . . . She rocked the little thing to sleep, washed the dishes, and got our supper." The landlady, continued Anthony, gave her guests her own "warm bedroom," and at 6:00 A.M., prepared them a huge breakfast.

"Now for the moral of this story," Anthony concluded. "When we came to pay our bill, the dolt of a husband took the money and put it in his pocket. He had not lifted a hand to lighten that woman's burdens, but had sat and talked with the men in the bar room. . . . Yet the law gives him the right to every dollar she earns, and when she needs two cents to buy a darning needle she has to ask him and explain what she wants it for."

Anthony interrupted her tour to bring a stack of newly signed petitions to the February 1855 session of the state legislature. When the lawmakers once again turned deaf ears to her appeal, she returned to her travels. Then she received a tempting offer. The American Anti-Slavery Society, headed by fervent abolitionist William Lloyd Garrison, offered her a job as its agent in New York State.

Anthony had long yearned for a chance to strike a blow at slavery, and this seemed like a perfect opportunity. Furthermore, the society offered a small salary, which meant she would

Elizabeth Stanton shows off one of her sons in 1850. Anthony loved Stanton's children, but she thought "baby-making" claimed too much of her friend's time.

"The ladies," he said, "always have the best place and the choicest tidbit at the table. They have the best seats in the cars, carriages, and sleighs. . . . They have their choice on which side of the bed they will lie. . . . A lady's dress costs three times as much as that of a gentleman; and at the present time, with the prevailing fashion, one lady occupies three times as much space in the world as a gentleman. . . . If there is any inequality or oppression in the case, the gentlemen are the sufferers."

The chairman went on to discuss husbands who had signed Anthony's petitions. To cover such cases, he smilingly recommended a law authorizing wives to exchange clothes with their spouses. Then, he said, "the husband may wear petticoats, and the wife breeches, and thus indicate to their neighbors and the public the true relation in which they stand to each other." The speech was received, according to reporters, "with roars of laughter."

Anthony may have been closer to tears than laughter, but she did not give up. She continued to make speeches, write letters, and knock on doors, enduring snowstorms, heat waves, public ridicule, and personal insult from both men and women. After four more years of campaigning, she and Stanton composed a powerful speech, which the eloquent Stanton delivered to the New York State legis-

not have to rely on donations in order to live. After considering Garrison's proposal, however, she turned it down. She knew what she had to do, and she was soon back on the road with her women's-rights petitions. In February 1856, as she had promised, she reappeared at the legislative session with an imposing pile of signed petitions requesting changes in the laws. This time the response was given by the chairman of the Senate Judiciary Committee.

lature on March 19, 1860. The following day, New York State had a new law.

The Married Woman's Property Act gave wives control over wages they earned and property they inherited, "not subject to control or interference" by their husbands. It allowed them to engage in lawsuits under their own names and to make contracts and investments. It also provided that "every married woman shall be joint guardian of her children with her husband, with equal powers regarding them."

Passage of the New York bill quickly led to similar laws in other states, profoundly affecting the lives of millions of Americans. The bill had cost a decade of relentless struggle, but it had swept away legal injustices that had prevailed for a thousand years. It was an extraordinary victory. The battle for women's rights, however, was far from over.

A flag flies above the state capitol in Albany, New York, scene of Anthony and Stanton's long but ultimately successful campaign for women's property rights.

Abraham Lincoln "freed" the Confederacy's slaves in 1863, but because his Emancipation Proclamation could not be enforced in the rebel states, it had no immediate effect.

FIVE

Crisis Years

By 1860, the American women's movement was emerging as a potent force, but its achievements were soon to be overshadowed by violent civil conflict. Regional tension had long been a fact of American political life, with the North, South, and West competing for federal funds, favorable trade laws, and power. From the 1850s on, the issue creating the sharpest sectional conflict was slavery.

Many people, Southerners in particular, believed slavery should be permitted in the western territories that had not yet joined the Union; others, many of them Northerners, thought it should be prohibited except in states where it was already legal. A third faction, the abolitionists, considered slavery morally wrong and demanded its immediate end in all U.S. lands.

Anthony had long wanted to aid the abolition cause. She had turned down the American Anti-Slavery Society's job offer in order to continue her petition-gathering tour, but then the slavery conflict accelerated and even affected her own family directly. Merritt Anthony, Susan's 22-year-old brother, had settled in Osawatomie, Kansas. Because the inhabitants of the territory had been given the right to decide whether or not Kansas would permit slavery, the territory had become the scene of bloody battles between pro- and antislavery factions. In May 1856, a proslavery mob killed five antislavery leaders in the town of Lawrence, Kansas. In retaliation, John Brown, a fanatical abolitionist, led a raid in which five proslavery settlers were killed. The cycle of violence continued when pro-

John Brown receives a farewell kiss as he goes to the gallows. The fiery abolitionist was hanged after leading a bloody raid on Harpers Ferry, Virginia, in 1859.

slavery men attacked Osawatomie and killed 30 of its 50 inhabitants.

For days, the Anthony family did not know whether Merritt was dead or alive. When news of his safety finally reached them, Susan wrote to her brother. "Words cannot tell," she said, "how often we think of you or how sadly we feel that the terrible crime of this nation against humanity [slavery] is being avenged on the heads of our sons and brothers." Merritt's narrow escape brought the issue of slavery into sharp focus for Susan Anthony. At this point, she received an interesting letter.

"The Anti-Slavery Society wants you in the field," it said. "We need your earnestness, your practical talent, your energy, and perseverance.... We want your cheerfulness, your spirit—in short, yourself." Anthony responded quickly. "I shall be very glad," she said, "if I am able to render even the most humble service to this cause." Putting her in charge of all its operations in New York State, the society wrote, "We want your name to all letters and your hand in all arrangements. We like your form of posters; by all means let 'No Union With Slaveholders' be conspicuous upon them."

In the days before radio and television, the most effective way to bring a message to the public was to make personal appearances. Assigned to increase sympathy for the antislavery society's goals among the people of New York, Anthony organized a small army of speakers, deploying them around the state with almost military precision. She enlisted the services of both men and women, some of them prominent abolitionists, some of them former slaves. She mapped out their routes, arranged transportation, hired halls, and arranged advance publicity for their appearances. Beyond assuming responsibility for the campaign's operations, she scheduled a grueling series of lectures for herself.

Speaking on behalf of temperance and women's rights, Anthony had often faced ridicule; now she confronted outright hostility from many audiences. Americans had strong sentiments about slavery. Even the moderates, who hoped to limit the expansion of slavery, deeply opposed the abolitionists and their slogan, "No Union With Slaveholders." Such a policy, the moderates felt, could lead to the breakup of the United States.

Anthony, who was often joined by Elizabeth Stanton during her antislavery tours, had no trouble attracting audiences, but she frequently had trouble being heard. On a number of occasions, mobs of angry antiabolitionists invaded halls where she was speaking, drowning her out with shouts and catcalls. Sometimes she was pelted with rotten eggs.

In Syracuse, a screaming crowd labeled a mannequin "Susan B. Anthony," dragged it to the town center, and burned it. In Albany, the mayor was prepared for trouble. Before the speeches, he took a seat on the platform, placed his loaded revolver on his knee, and stared at the audience. Then he told Anthony to open the meeting. It proceeded without interruption.

Despite the hostility of many of her audiences, Anthony began to speak with new power and conviction, frequently telling her listeners things they did not want to hear. "The men and women of the North are slave-holders,

A mid-1850s poster offers a 20-year-old black woman, "valued at $900," as a raffle prize. Such blatant abuses increased support for the abolition movement.

those of the South slave-owners. The guilt rests on the North equally with the South," she said. "We ask you to feel as if you, yourselves, were the slaves. . . . We demand the abolition of slavery because the slave is a human being, and because man should not hold property in his fellow man. . . . We preach revolution!"

Although she was deeply involved in the antislavery movement, Anthony remained fiercely committed to the struggle for women's rights. At a state teachers' convention in 1857, she pre-

William Lloyd Garrison criticized Anthony for helping a Boston woman escape from her abusive husband; she criticized him for failing to understand women's rights.

rose, pointed dramatically at Anthony, and thundered, "Do you mean to say you want the boys and girls to room side by side in dormitories? To educate them together can have but one result!"

Even though women far outnumbered men at the teachers' convention, Anthony's motion for coeducation was voted down by a huge majority. Shortly afterward, she received a sympathetic letter from Stanton. "What an infernal set of fools those schoolmarms must be!" she wrote. "Well, if in order to please men they wish to live on air, let them. The sooner the present generation of women dies out, the better. We have idiots enough in the world now without such women propagating any more." Calming down, she noted that she and Anthony would outlast the "set of fools": "We shall not be in our prime before 50, and after that we shall be good for 20 years at least."

For the next three years, Anthony continued to work for both women's rights and the abolition of slavery. In May 1860, 2 months after steering the Married Women's Property Act through the New York State legislature, she attended the 10th annual National Woman's Rights Convention, held in New York City. (Almost every year since the 1848 Seneca Falls gathering, suffragists had met to discuss issues of pressing concern.) Here, Stanton's radical views once again created an uproar.

sented a resolution proposing that all American schools "open their doors to woman and give her equal and identical educational advantages side by side with her brother man."

The proposal created an immediate uproar. Coeducation, declared its opponents, was "a vast social evil" that would "destroy the balance of nature." The state superintendent of schools

Stanton had long been a fierce opponent of divorce laws that in most states made it almost impossible for women to end their marriages, even in cases of proven abuse. At the New York convention, she proposed a resolution that would have named drunkenness, desertion, and cruelty as legal grounds for divorce. A wave of disapproval swept through the crowded hall, for current opinion held the ties of marriage as permanent as the bond between parents and children.

Most of the delegates, including several of Anthony and Stanton's close male associates and supporters—abolitionists who up to this point had stood firmly behind the women's rights movement—opposed the resolutions, and the convention voted to adjourn without endorsing them. Criticizing Anthony for backing them, an abolitionist clergyman said, "You are not married. You have no business to be discussing marriage." Anthony responded with impeccable logic. "Well," she said, "you are not a slave. Suppose you quit lecturing on slavery."

A few months later, Anthony's support for women's rights again brought her into sharp conflict with her abolitionist associates, in this case Wendell Phillips and William Lloyd Garrison. One December night, while visiting Lydia Mott in Albany, Anthony opened the door to find a heavily veiled woman waiting to see her. Introducing herself as the wife of Massachusetts state senator Charles Phelps, she told Anthony a shocking story.

When she had presented her husband with evidence of his infidelities, he had knocked her down a flight of stairs and then committed her to an insane asylum. After a year and a half she had finally won her freedom and a visit with one of her children. Unable to bear the thought of being separated again from her daughter, who by law belonged to her husband, Phelps had abducted the little girl and come to Anthony for help.

Anthony promptly took Phelps and her daughter on the train to New York City and found them refuge with a Quaker friend who had hidden fugitive slaves. On her return to Albany, Anthony faced not only threats of arrest from Senator Phelps but outraged protests from William Lloyd Garrison, who feared that her action could harm the antislavery crusade. Calling her assistance to Phelps "hasty and ill-judged, no matter how well-meant," he asked, "Don't you know that the law of Massachusetts gives the father . . . control of the children?"

Furious, Anthony replied, "Yes I know it. Does the law of the United States not give the slaveholder the ownership of the slave? And don't you break it every time you help a slave to Canada? Well, the law which gives the father the sole ownership of the children is just as wicked and I'll break it just as quickly. You would die before

Looters watch a "colored orphanage" burn during Manhattan's 1863 draft riots. Hundreds of blacks were killed or injured during the city's three days of murderous violence.

you would deliver a slave to his master, and I will die before I will give up that child to its father."

Garrison was totally committed to obtaining freedom for black people, but this was the second time he had failed to recognize the need for women's freedom. His lack of understanding puzzled Anthony. "Very many abolitionists," she commented in her diary, "have yet to learn the ABC of women's rights."

Meanwhile, the conflict over slavery had come to a head. In February 1861, soon after Abraham Lincoln's election to the presidency, the seven states of the lower South withdrew from the Union to form the Confederate States of America. In April, the Confederate Army opened fire on Fort Sumter, South Carolina; the Civil War had begun. In spite of the conflict, Anthony believed that the battle for women's rights should proceed. Her efforts to organize a convention in 1861, however, failed; America's mind was on the war.

In 1862, while the nation's attentions lay elsewhere, the New York State legislature revoked some of the rights it had granted women under the Married Women's Property Act. Feeling betrayed, Anthony wrote to to her friend Lydia Mott. "We deserve to suffer for our confidence in 'man's sense of justice,'" she said. "I am sick at heart, but cannot carry the world against the wish and will of our best friends." Personal sorrow deepened her sense of desolation: In late 1862 her father became suddenly ill and died. To the grief-stricken Anthony, "it seemed as if everything in the world must stop."

But she could not stop for long. Her interest in the world revived in 1863 when Lincoln issued his Emancipation Proclamation, which ordered freedom for slaves in the rebellious Southern states. Because it did not affect slaves in states that remained within the Union, the proclamation failed to satisfy many abolitionists, including Anthony. In her diary, she wrote, "To forever blot out slavery is the only possible compensation for this merciless war."

To arouse public sentiment for full emancipation, Anthony and Stanton decided to start a new organization, the Women's National Loyal League. Its mission would be to mobilize support for a constitutional amendment outlawing slavery. Recalling the success of her petitions in winning the women's property law, Anthony envisioned a new campaign. She and Stan-

A wounded Civil War veteran offers a crisp salute. Surprising many racist Union officers, black soldiers demonstrated great courage under fire.

ton would deliver to Congress the largest petition in American history.

The prospect of hard work helped Anthony cope with her grief over her father's death. After renting an office in New York City (where Stanton and her family now lived), she sent out thousands of letters to the nation's women. "There must be a law abolishing slavery," she wrote. "Women, you can-

Former slaves learn to read and write. Anthony believed that the education of the nation's black population should be America's highest postwar priority.

not vote or fight for your country. Your only way to be a power in the government is through the exercise of this one, sacred constitutional 'right of petition,' and we ask you to use it now to the utmost."

As Anthony was sending out her letters, New York City was becoming an increasingly dangerous place. Support for the war was far from universal, and in 1863, when the federal government announced its plans to draft men into the army, riots broke out. The principal targets of the mobs' fury were

those considered responsible for the war: blacks and abolitionists. In the worst of these so-called draft riots, hundreds of black people were killed or wounded. Abolitionists' homes and shops were burned and looted, and the offices of Horace Greeley's antislavery newspaper, the New York *Tribune*, were destroyed. "These are terrible times," said Anthony in a letter to her family—but she kept right on working.

By early 1864, she had collected an amazing 400,000 signatures; in April, the U.S. Senate passed the Thirteenth

Amendment, which said that "neither slavery nor involuntary servitude . . . shall exist within the United States." Assured that approval by the House of Representatives would soon follow, Anthony and Stanton dissolved the Women's National Loyal League. Anthony decided that when the war ended, she would work toward the education and employment training of the nation's newly liberated black men and women.

Anthony resented Northerners who worried about "dealing" with emancipated slaves. "What arrogance in *us*," she said, "to put the question, What shall *we* do with a race of men and women who have fed, clothed, and supported both themselves and their oppressors for centuries!" She counseled white Americans to "treat the Negroes just as you do the Irish, the Scotch, and the Germans. Educate them to all the blessings of our free institutions, to our schools and churches, to every department of industry, trade, and art."

After spending a few months with her family in Rochester, the 43-year-old Anthony was anxious to begin what she called "the reconstruction of the Nation on the broad basis of justice and equality." Reconstruction, however, would have to wait until the war ended. In 1864, when her brother Daniel sent her a railroad ticket and an invitation to visit him and his wife in Kansas, she accepted eagerly.

Daniel Anthony was the mayor of Leavenworth, a bustling city whose population had grown from 4,000 to 22,000 in 8 years. Susan Anthony liked

Cheering wildly, abolitionist congressmen celebrate passage of the Thirteenth Amendment, which abolished slavery in the United States, on January 31, 1865.

Pedestrians and horses traverse the unpaved main street of a Kansas city in the 1860s. Anthony, who visited the state in 1864, considered settling there.

Kansas and its inhabitants, but she was appalled by their prejudice against blacks, thousands of whom had settled in the state. Anthony, who had been longing "to go out and do battle for the Lord once more," decided that here was work cut out for her. Thinking about staying on in Kansas, she visited "colored" schools and churches, talked to black leaders, and helped organize an Equal Rights League for blacks.

Then a series of news bulletins arrived. On April 9, 1865, Confederate General Robert E. Lee surrendered to Union General Ulysses S. Grant, the commander in chief of the Union Army. Five days later, Abraham Lincoln was mortally wounded by an assassin. The president was dead, but the war was over; now the reconstruction of the nation could begin. Anthony had been eager to help obtain civil rights for blacks, but she was not comforted by reports about the postwar activities of the abolitionist movement.

Believing suffrage for black men to be the most important issue, many of Anthony's former colleagues now concentrated exclusively on that goal, at the expense of the struggle for woman suffrage. As one of her good friends, abolitionist leader Wendell Phillips, put it, "I would not mix the movements. . . . I think such mixture would lose for the Negro far more than we should gain for the woman." Unless some drastic changes were made, black and white men would have the vote; black and white women would not.

Members of a black pioneer family gather outside their midwestern home. Anthony was shocked by the racist attitudes of many whites in Kansas, where thousands of blacks had settled.

Anthony received an urgent appeal from Parker Pillsbury, an ardent abolitionist and longtime supporter of rights for women. "Why have you deserted the field of action at a time like this?" he asked. "If you are absent, who is to make the plea for woman?" Elizabeth Stanton's plea to Anthony was even more direct. "Come home," she wrote. Anthony hesitated. Then she read that the proposed Fourteenth Amendment referred to voters as "*male* citizens." Packing her bags, she headed east.

Anthony had spent years fighting for abolition, but she angered many of the movement's members by demanding votes for women as well as for blacks.

Revolution

Until the Fourteenth Amendment was written, the word *male* had never been used in the Constitution to define those entitled to vote. Women's right to vote had been denied by tradition and state law alone. Anthony and Stanton regarded the amendment's wording, which specifically excluded females, as an enormous step backward, and they began to campaign against its passage.

During the Civil War, the women's-rights movement had ground to a halt; the Women's Rights Convention of 1866 was the first to be held since 1860. Anthony and Stanton hoped that at this meeting, they could both reaffirm the movement's concern for black suffrage and reawaken its interest in suffrage for women. Addressing a large audience at the convention's opening session, Anthony proposed that the society direct its future efforts toward securing voting rights for all American adults, black and white, male and female.

"We wish to broaden our women's rights platform," she said, "and make it in name what it ever has been in spirit, a human rights platform. As women we can no longer . . . work in two separate movements to get the ballot for the two disfranchised classes, Negroes and women." After suggesting that the Women's Rights Association concentrate its forces on "one grand, distinctive idea—universal suffrage," she moved that it rename itself the American Equal Rights Society. Her motion was unanimously approved, but not before several members had objected, asserting that the society should focus solely on securing voting rights for blacks.

Newspaper publisher Horace Greeley had been an early supporter of the women's movement, but he abandoned it in 1866. Women, he said, needed babies, not votes.

Wendell Phillips, again arguing that the fight for woman suffrage would weaken the cause of black suffrage, insisted that the word *male* would have to stay in the Fourteenth Amendment, at least for the time being. Anthony, who had dedicated years of her life to the antislavery movement, had been among the first to endorse votes for blacks. Nevertheless, she responded to Phillips's words with characteristic firmness. "I would sooner cut off my right hand," she said, "than ask for the ballot for the black man and not for woman."

Even newspaper publisher Horace Greeley, once a trusted ally of the women's movement, abandoned the cause of woman suffrage. What a woman needed, he said in the New York *Tribune*, was not a vote but a "wicker-work cradle and a dimple-cheeked baby." Furthermore, he asserted, most women did not even want the vote. To this argument, Anthony responded, "So they told us when we said the Negro ought to be free; he did not wish it; he was contented and happy. As we replied relative to the Negro, so do we regarding women."

The New York State Constitution was scheduled for revision in 1867. When the newly formed Equal Rights Association requested that women be allowed to vote on the changes, negative rumbles were heard across the state. Most outspoken and contemptuous were the comments of the New York *World*. "Parker Pillsbury, one of the notabilities of the body," sneered the newspaper, "is a good-looking white man naturally, but he has a cowed and sneakish expression stealing over him, as though he regretted he had not been born a nigger or one of these females."

The *World* described Anthony as "lean, cadaverous, and intellectual, with the proportions of a file and the voice of a hurdy-gurdy [barrel organ]." The other members of the association, said the paper, were "mummified and fossilated females, void of domestic duties, habits, and natural affections"; "crack-brained, rheumatic, dyspeptic, henpecked men"; and "self-educated, oily-faced, insolent, gabbling Negroes."

Congress passed the Fourteenth Amendment in June 1866. As with all amendments to the Constitution, the next step was ratification, or approval, by three-fourths of the states. Anthony and Stanton now assigned themselves two goals: to block ratification of the amendment by the New York State legislature and to secure the vote for women in the new state constitution. Hoping to reconvert Horace Greeley to their cause, they asked him to publicize woman suffrage along with black suffrage. Their appeal failed. Greeley, recalled Stanton later, said, "No! You must not get up any agitation for that measure. . . . This is the Negro's hour."

Anthony and Stanton, of course, believed it was also the *women's* hour. Once again they made speeches, wrote letters, and circulated petitions. Addressing the state constitutional convention, Anthony predicted that one day, women would serve on juries and in the armed forces. Greeley, a delegate at the convention, laughed. "If you vote, are you ready to fight?" he asked. "Yes, Mr. Greeley," snapped Anthony,

When suffragist Lucy Stone married Henry Blackwell, she shocked her contemporaries—but not her suffragist husband—by demanding to be called "Mrs. Stone."

"just as you fought in the late war—at the point of a goose-quill [pen]!"

Despite the efforts of Anthony, Stanton, and their colleagues, New York eventually ratified the Fourteenth Amendment and, in its new constitution, gave the vote exclusively to men. The woman suffragists had lost a battle. But they had no intention of losing the war.

As the New York State campaign was being waged, another was under way in the West. Anthony and Stanton's friend Lucy Stone had been traveling through Kansas, mobilizing support for amendments that would give blacks and women the right to vote at the state level. The Kansas Republican party,

Women of Leavenworth, Kansas, distribute campaign literature in 1867. Despite the efforts of Anthony and her colleagues, Kansans voted against woman suffrage.

along with such influential East Coast newspapers as Horace Greeley's *Tribune,* supported only the black-suffrage amendment, once again calling on women to wait for the vote.

When Stone returned to the East Coast in the spring of 1867, she told Anthony that the Kansas woman-suffrage amendment was in danger. Without further strenuous campaigning, she said, it faced defeat in the state's November elections. In August, accompanied by Stanton, Anthony boarded a train and headed for Kansas. There, the two women lined up a series of lectures, crisscrossing the rugged countryside in horse-drawn wagons. In a letter to her family, Anthony said, "We speak in school-houses, barns, sawmills, log cabins with boards for seats and lanterns hung around for lights, but people come 20 miles to hear us."

Not even Anthony and Stanton, however, could match the forces ranged against their cause. Intensely concerned about securing the loyalty of future black voters, the national Republican party was pouring money into Kansas. The party's efforts, enthusiastically supported by the eastern press, aimed not only at winning black suffrage, but at defeating the woman-suffrage amendment. Then, in October, Anthony and Stanton got help from an unexpected source.

Their new ally was George Francis Train, a wealthy, eccentric railroad financier and an ardent believer in voting rights for women. In October, he sent a telegram offering to stump the state for equal rights and woman suffrage. Anthony had never met Train, but she accepted without hesitation. "Come to Kansas," she wired back. "The people want you, the women want you."

Train promptly joined the suffragists, adding a note of glamour to their campaign. Tall, elegantly dressed, and supremely self-confident, he delighted Kansas audiences with his theatrical style and dramatic speeches. Even initially hostile listeners cheered his colorful attacks on Republicans and his appeals to male gallantry. "Every man in Kansas," he would shout, who votes against giving women the vote "has insulted his mother, his daughter, his sister and his wife!"

At first astonished by Train's flamboyance, Anthony and Stanton came to respect and admire their hardworking supporter. Their alliance with him, however, horrified their abolitionist colleagues back East. Most abolitionists were now associated with the Republican party, which championed

George Francis Train provided Anthony and Stanton with welcome assistance in Kansas, but eastern abolitionists considered him a political liability.

black suffrage. Train not only belonged to the Democratic party—the political organization associated with Southern slaveholders—but he firmly opposed enfranchising blacks before women. Some of his detractors considered him a racist.

In the end, not even the combined eloquence of Anthony, Stanton, and Train saved the day. Thirty thousand Kansans cast votes on election day. Ten thousand of them voted for the black-suffrage amendment and 9,000 supported the woman-suffrage amendment. Both motions lost by a

Financed by eccentric millionaire George Francis Train and edited by Elizabeth Cady Stanton, The Revolution *began publication on January 8, 1868.*

two-to-one margin, but the outcome was not a complete defeat. On this, the first occasion in American history in which woman suffrage had been submitted to the electorate, almost one-third of the voters had approved it.

Blaming the defeat of the Kansas black-suffrage amendment on "that crack-brained harlequin and semi-lunatic," George Train, the eastern abolitionists warned Anthony and Stanton to stay away from him. Nevertheless, when Train offered to finance

a cross-country woman-suffrage lecture tour, they accepted. Then he asked Anthony why she and Stanton were not publishing an equal-rights newspaper. She told him they had long dreamed of such a project, but they could not afford it. He replied, she recalled later, "Well, I will give you the money." She thought he was joking.

At a woman-suffrage meeting the following night, Train mounted the podium. "Ladies and gentlemen, I have an announcement to make," he said. "When Miss Anthony gets back to New York, she is going to start a woman-suffrage paper. Its name is to be *The Revolution*; its motto, 'Men, their rights, and nothing more; Women, their rights, and nothing less.' This paper is to be a weekly, price $2 a year; its editors, Elizabeth Cady Stanton and Parker Pillsbury; its proprietor, Susan B. Anthony. Let everybody subscribe for it!"

Obviously, Train had meant what he said. Anthony and Stanton decided to accept his offer, even though they knew it would further infuriate the abolitionists. What did that matter, they reasoned, when the abolitionists had already deemed the cause of woman suffrage a lesser concern? After lecturing on women's rights in every large city between Kansas and the East Coast, Anthony and Stanton set up an office in New York City. In her final diary entry for 1867, Anthony wrote, "The year goes out, and never did one depart that had been so filled with earnest and effective work; 9,000 votes for women in Kansas, and a newspaper started! *The Revolution* is going to be work, work, and more work. The old out and the new in!"

Carrying a new slogan on its masthead—"Principle, not Policy; Justice, not Favors"—the first issue of *The Revolution* was published on January 8, 1868. The appearance of the paper drew the usual patronizing criticism from conservatives. The *New York Times*, accusing Stanton of "leaving her own houschold in a neglected condition," said, "Every woman has a natural and inalienable right to a good husband and a pretty baby. When, by proper 'agitation,' she has secured this right, she best honors herself and her sex by leaving public affairs behind her."

Train, a man of many—and often short-lived—enthusiasms, left for England soon after the first issue of *The Revolution* appeared. He resumed his financial support of the paper when he returned almost a year later, but in the meantime, Anthony was responsible for financing the paper. Although she augmented its slender revenues by lecturing for money, its debts continued to mount. Nevertheless, it continued to roll off the presses.

The Revolution made its points in the clear, strong voice of its editors. Rejecting the abolitionist and Republican position, it repudiated the Four-

Abolitionist Harriet Beecher Stowe, author of Uncle Tom's Cabin, *refused to write for* The Revolution *unless its name was changed to something "less aggressive."*

teenth Amendment and called for suffrage for blacks *and* women. During the two years of its existence, the newspaper addressed a variety of other issues, many of them hotly controversial. It discussed prostitution, the inequity of contemporary divorce laws, society's double standard for the sexes and discriminatory treatment of women, and the need for stronger labor unions and better working conditions.

The Revolution also reflected Anthony's concern for working women. Among the first to endorse the then-revolutionary concept of equal pay for equal work, she demanded that the printers who produced *The Revolution* hire women typesetters. Organizing a group called the Workingwomen's Association, she counseled its members once a week in her office. "Make up your minds to take the lean with the fat, and be early and late at the case precisely as men are," she told women typesetters. "Scorn to be coddled by your employers; make them understand that you are in their service as workers, not as women."

The newspaper had a core of loyal readers, but its radical approach frightened as many people as it attracted. When, for example, Anthony and Stanton asked Harriet Beecher Stowe to write an article for *The Revolution*, the celebrated author of *Uncle Tom's Cabin* agreed—but only if the editors would agree to rename the publication. *The True Republic* was suggested as an appropriate substitute.

Anthony asked Stanton what she thought of Stowe's request. "I should consider it a great mistake," replied Stanton. "You and I have not forgotten the conflict of the last 20 years—the ridicule, persecution, denunciation, detraction. . . . A journal called *Rosebud* might answer for those who come with kid gloves and perfumes to lay [flowers] on the monuments which in sweat and tears we have built; but for us . . . there is no name but *The Revolution*."

Searching for new subscribers, Anthony went to Washington, D.C. After signing up several congressmen, she marched into the office of President Andrew Johnson himself. The Republican leader, she later reported, said he was not interested in her paper. "Mr. Johnson," she replied, "Mrs. Stanton and myself for two years have boldly told the Republican party that they must give ballots to women as well as Negroes, and by means of *The Revolution* we are bound to drive the party to this logical conclusion or break it into a thousand pieces." This, she recalled with satisfaction, "brought him to his pocketbook." He signed his name quickly, "as much as to say, 'Anything to get rid of this woman!'"

The Revolution was an excellent publication, well written and clearly printed. Nevertheless, it came to be a financial burden too great for Anthony to bear, and in 1870, she sadly gave it up. "It was like signing my own death warrant," she said in a letter to a friend. Anthony's early biographers reported that she kept bound copies of the newspaper for the rest of her life, often reading and rereading its pages.

Meanwhile, the battle over suffrage continued. To reinforce the Fourteenth Amendment, abolitionists and Republicans introduced the Fifteenth Amendment, which included the words, "The right of citizens of the United States to vote shall not be denied or abridged . . . on account of race, color, or previous condition of servitude." The amendment omitted the word *sex*, which would have extended the franchise to women. Anthony petitioned Congress to add the crucial word, but her efforts were unsuccessful. Most congressmen believed that giving women the vote would give them undue and unnatural power over men. Woman suffrage, said one senator, would "make every home a hell on earth."

Undeterred, Anthony and Stanton next persuaded a sympathetic congressman to introduce an amendment basing suffrage solely on citizenship. Dated March 1869, it was the first woman-suffrage amendment ever proposed. Its path to final approval would be long and steep.

Anthony and Stanton continued to press their case at the 1869 American Equal Rights Association Convention. Some of the delegates, particularly those from the new states of the West, agreed that woman suffrage should go hand in hand with black suffrage. Most of the delegates, however, voiced their strong support of the Fifteenth Amendment. Reasserting their conviction that woman suffrage would have to wait, they sharply criticized Anthony and Stanton for insisting it have priority. Much to the two women's disappointment, even such friends as Lucy Stone, Lydia Mott, and Amelia Bloomer voted with the majority.

After the convention recessed, a delegate from Illinois told Anthony she considered the Equal Rights Associa-

President Andrew Johnson told Anthony he did not wish to subscribe to The Revolution, *but when she refused to take no for an answer he signed up.*

tion a fraud. "I would not have come," she said, "nor would any of us, if we had known what it was. We supposed we were coming to a woman suffrage convention." The woman from Illinois was not alone. Calling together other like-minded delegates, Anthony proposed that they form a new organization.

With the enthusiastic cooperation of women from 19 of the nation's 32 states, the National Woman Suffrage Association was born. Stanton would be its president, Anthony a member of its executive board. Its goal: passage of a constitutional amendment granting women the right to vote.

Anthony was distressed by the 1869 split in the women's rights movement, but she remained optimistic. The crusade for suffrage, she said, "cannot be damaged."

SEVEN

Division

After Anthony and her supporters resigned from the Equal Rights Association, the American women's movement split. "I think we need two national associations for women," announced Lucy Stone, "so that those who do not oppose the Fifteenth Amendment ... may yet have an organization with which they can work in harmony." She wanted, she said, "to unite those who cannot use the methods which Mrs. Stanton and Susan use."

Unlike Stone, Anthony and Stanton not only called for woman suffrage, they demanded radical changes in society. Stone and her followers believed that the women's-vote cause was injured by such militant views and preferred to work with male associates on a more moderate course.

Led by Stone, the conservatives formed their own group, the American Woman Suffrage Association. Its first convention, announced Stone, would be held in Cleveland, Ohio, in November 1869. Neither Anthony nor Stanton was invited to the meeting, although such old friends as Lydia Mott and Amelia Bloomer planned to attend. "Can it be possible that a National Woman's Suffrage Convention is called without Susan's knowledge or consent?" asked the astonished Rochester *Democrat*. "A National Woman's Suffrage Association without speeches from Susan B. Anthony and Mrs. Stanton will be a new order of things. The idea seems absurd."

Anthony and Stanton agreed. For decades they had been the backbone of the crusade for woman suffrage;

now that success seemed within reach, they were appalled to think it could be weakened by a feud. "If I am a stumbling block," said Stanton, "I will gladly resign my office. Having fought the world for 20 years, I do not wish to turn and fight those who have so long stood together."

Invited or not, Anthony decided to attend the convention, prepared to give up her new organization if its existence threatened the cause. Her appearance at the meeting prompted a roar of applause, and she soon asked permission to speak. After expressing her hope that the new organization would "go in strong array . . . to demand a Sixteenth Amendment to the Constitution," she made an emotional appeal to the delegates.

"So help me, heaven!" she said. "I care not what may come out of this convention, so that this great cause shall go forward to its consummation! And though this convention . . . nullify the National Association of which I am a member . . . if you will do the work in Washington so that this amendment will be proposed, and will go with me to the several legislatures and *compel* them to adopt it, I will thank God for this convention as long as I have the breath of life!"

The delegates cheered Anthony's words, but they rejected her plea. Instead of concentrating on obtaining a woman-suffrage amendment to the Constitution, they voted to work for suffrage on a local level, state by state. The women's association then elected a man, the prominent minister Henry Ward Beecher, as its president. The animosity between Anthony and Stone was now out in the open, deepening the rift in the women's movement and forcing supporters to take sides. Nevertheless, Anthony was determined to press on. "The movement cannot be damaged," she said in a letter to a friend. "The wheels are secure on the iron rails, and no 'National' or 'American' . . . can block them. Individuals may jump on or off, yet the train is stopped thereby but for a moment."

Although its progress was slow, the "train" was rolling. In 1869, the territory of Wyoming (which would become a state in 1890) gave its women the right to vote, to hold office, and to serve on juries. Partly to celebrate this victory, and partly to acknowledge Anthony's 50th birthday, a group of New York City suffragists decided to give a small party in 1870. The affair snowballed, drawing a huge crowd of admirers as well as unusually friendly newspaper coverage.

The New York *Herald* headlined its story "Susan's Half Century," the *World* called her "the Moses of her sex," and the *Sun*, its editors probably intending to be complimentary, labeled her "a brave old maid." Even Horace Greeley's usually critical *Tribune* bestowed a few grudging words of praise. "We have often felt

Wyoming Territory women—who in 1869 became the first enfranchised females in the world—line up to vote in Cheyenne.

Victoria Woodhull, a flamboyant campaigner for women's rights and a variety of other causes, became one of Susan B. Anthony's most unlikely allies.

[that her] methods were as unwise as we thought her aims undesirable," noted the paper. "But through these years of disputation and struggling, Miss Anthony has thoroughly impressed friends and enemies alike with the sincerity and earnestness of her purpose."

Deeply moved by the tributes of her friends at the birthday party, Anthony rose to speak. "If this were an assembled mob opposing the rights of women," she began, "I should know what to say." Then, true to form, she made an impassioned speech for the rights of women. After the party, she wrote in her diary, "Fiftieth birthday! One half-century done, one score years of it hard labor for . . . temperance—emancipation—enfranchisement—oh, such a struggle!" Writing to a friend about the occasion, she said, "I am so glad of it all, because it will teach the young girls that to be true to principle—to live an idea, though an unpopular one—that to live single—without any man's name—may be honorable."

When Anthony gave up publishing *The Revolution*, the newspaper was $10,000 in debt. Friends had urged her to cancel the debt by declaring bankruptcy, but she had replied, "My pride for women, to say nothing of my conscience, says no." In order to raise money, she spent most of 1870 on a speech-making tour of the Midwest. During this trip, she met Francis Minor, a St. Louis lawyer whose political ideas would deeply affect her own.

The U.S. Constitution, argued the Missourian, gave the states authority to make voting rules, but it did not give them the authority to prohibit a citizen from voting. Because the Fourteenth Amendment specifically said that no state could "abridge the privileges . . . of citizens," Minor contended, and because women were citizens, they had the right to vote. Why not, he asked Anthony, test this theory in the next election?

Minor's ideas were much on Anthony's mind in early 1871, while she prepared for the annual woman-suffrage convention in Washington, D.C. When she got there, she found the capital buzzing with gossip and speculation about a most unusual woman. She was Victoria C. Woodhull, a beautiful, strong-minded, and highly unconventional reformer. Woodhull would prove to be both a powerful ally and a heavy burden to Anthony and her colleagues.

An outspoken crusader for women's rights, Woodhull was also an advocate of socialism, spiritualism, and—shockingly, in the 19th century—"free love," the notion that sexual relations outside of marriage were morally acceptable. Woodhull and her sister, Tennessee Claflin, published *Woodhull and Claflin's Weekly*, a feminist newspaper that ran stories about such "unmentionable" subjects as communism, prostitution, birth control, and abortion. The *Weekly* had also endorsed an unusual candidate for the presidency of the United States: Victoria Woodhull.

Anthony and her associates were astonished to learn that Woodhull, who had been called "no lady" and a "painted Jezebel," had been invited to address a congressional committee about woman suffrage. They were also intrigued: What would such a woman say about this vital subject? When Woodhull spoke on Capitol Hill, Anthony and her friends were in the audience. What they saw was no "Jezebel." Here was a poised, 33-year-old

woman wearing an elegant silk dress and a small, feathered hat. What they heard—to Anthony's surprise—was a carefully constructed argument for woman suffrage very much like the one put forth by Francis Minor.

Greatly impressed, Anthony invited Woodhull to speak at the next woman-suffrage convention. There Woodhull gave a rousing speech, threatening revolt unless Congress gave women the right to vote. "We mean treason, we mean secession, and on a thousand times grander scale than was that of

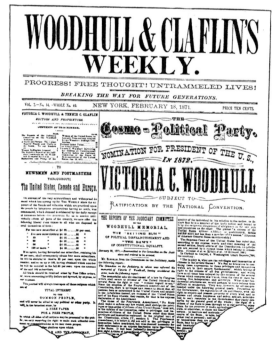

Each issue of Woodhull and Claflin's Weekly *carried its publishers' battle cry—"Progress! Free Thoughts! Untrammeled Lives!"—at the top of page one.*

the South," she proclaimed. "We are plotting revolution; we will overthrow this bogus republic and plant a government of righteousness in its stead!"

Inspired by Woodhull's fiery speech, the convention delegates passed a series of reform resolutions. One of them, which called for the repeal of all laws that interfered "with the rights of adult individuals to pursue happiness as they choose," created a furor among conservatives.

Asserting that the resolution was nothing less than an endorsement of free love, Lucy Stone and her followers claimed it would seriously damage the women's movement. Anthony's group, they said, was making a terrible mistake in associating with an "infamous" woman like Victoria Woodhull. Anthony was not alarmed. "I would welcome all the infamous women of New York," she said serenely, "if they would give speeches for freedom."

After the convention, Anthony embarked on another lecture tour, this one covering Wyoming, Utah, California, and Oregon. On December 31, she noted in her diary: "Thus closes 1871, a year full of hard work, six months east, six months west of the Rocky Mountains; 171 lectures, 13,000 miles of travel; gross receipts, $4,318; paid on

Wheat farmers tend their horses in Oregon, one of the territories Anthony visited on her 1871 lecture tour. In that year alone she traveled 13,000 miles.

An 1871 cartoon shows a heavily laden wife addressing Victoria Woodhull. "I'd rather travel the hardest path of matrimony," she says, "than follow your footsteps."

Clergyman Henry Ward Beecher, outraged when Woodhull published a shocking but true story about his love life, arranged to have her arrested on an obscenity charge.

debts, $2,271. Nothing ahead but to plod on." Plod on she did; her next speaking trip took her to Kansas, Nebraska, and Iowa. While there, she received disturbing news from the East.

In Anthony's absence, Victoria Woodhull had persuaded Stanton and other members of the National Woman Suffrage Association to back a new political party. Its presidential candidate in 1872 would be Woodhull herself. This plan, Anthony believed, would be a disaster. She and her allies had spent decades unsuccessfully seeking the vote for women; to expect men to *elect* a woman at this point struck her as absurd. "There is not a man who would vote a woman suffrage ticket," she wrote Stanton. Irritated by what she saw as Woodhull's concentration on her own interests, Anthony added, "she persistently means to run our craft into her port and no other."

Accompanied by a band of supporters, Woodhull made a surprise appearance at the 1872 meeting of the National Woman Suffrage Association.

When they moved that the association join forces with Woodhull's new party, Anthony declared them, as nonmembers, out of order. Then, ignoring their insistent demands to speak, she ordered the lights in the hall extinguished and adjourned the meeting. Woodhull was not invited to return.

A few weeks later, the newly formed Equal Rights party nominated Woodhull for president. Her campaign, however, was doomed. In November 1872, she published a true but scandalous story in her *Weekly* about a love affair between clergyman Henry Ward Beecher and another man's wife. In revenge, Beecher and his powerful friends arranged to have Woodhull and her sister arrested for publishing "obscene literature." By the time they were cleared of the charge, the election was over. Eventually, both sisters moved to England.

Anthony, too, was shortly to face arrest for her actions and convictions. Exercising what she claimed was her constitutional right, she voted in the 1872 election. After she was found guilty of casting an illegal ballot, she was ordered to pay a fine, which she refused to do. It was a daring and defiant gesture, but it failed in its objective; the court let her go free, bringing the case to an inconclusive halt.

Anthony was deeply disappointed, but a ray of hope remained.

Virginia Minor, wife of the St. Louis attorney who had urged Anthony to vote, had also cast a ballot in the 1872 election. When a St. Louis election inspector refused to register her, she and her husband sued him, arguing the case all the way to the U.S. Supreme Court.

In the end, Minor's case proved even more disappointing than Anthony's. When the Supreme Court handed down its decision in March 1875, it affirmed that women were citizens, but said that the *rights* of citizens were not defined by the Constitution. Voting rights, it said, were regulated solely by the states, not by the Constitution. The Fourteenth and Fifteenth Amendments did forbid discrimination—but only if it was based on race. Thus the argument that these amendments conferred suffrage on women was once and for all ruled invalid.

Woman suffrage had been defeated by Congress, by the Supreme Court, by both major political parties, by the male electorate. But nothing could defeat Susan Anthony. Now she recognized only one objective: passage of a constitutional amendment specifically granting women the right to vote. She would work for it for the rest of her life.

Stanton (left) and Anthony, one of the most remarkable teams in American history, confer on their book, History of Woman Suffrage, *in 1881.*

EIGHT

"The Fight Must Not Cease"

Unrelenting hard work characterized the next years of Anthony's life. She traveled through the western states and territories, building support for a woman-suffrage amendment to the Constitution and lecturing on such topics as "The Power of the Ballot." Earning about $100 per week from her speechmaking, she was slowly paying off her *Revolution* creditors. At last, on May 1, 1876, she wrote in her diary, "The day of the Jubilee for me has come. I have paid the last dollar of the *Revolution* debt!"

Anthony's settling of the debt was widely reported, receiving praise even from normally unsympathetic newspapers. "It seems to us—and we differ from her most emphatically on the question of woman suffrage—that her brave, unselfish life reflects a credit on womanhood," said the Utica *Observer*. The Chicago *Daily News* said that whatever her creditors might think of her political opinions, they would now "raise their hats in reverence" to her. Offering her what it must have considered the ultimate compliment, another paper said, "She has paid her debts like a man!"

Lectures by well-known people were popular in the days before radio, movies, and television. The public flocked to hear Anthony, whose activism had made her name a household word across the nation. Life on the road, however, was not easy. Traveling from one windy, desolate prairie town to another, Anthony spent much of her time waiting for trains in chilly railroad stations or sitting alone in hotel rooms, writing to her mother and sisters in

Ellsworth, Kansas, was typical of the remote western towns where Anthony spoke. She used her lecture fees to pay off her debts from the defunct Revolution.

Rochester. She rarely complained, but gourmet meals were rare on the frontier, and she did mention yearning for "a Christian cup of coffee."

In 1876, Anthony was back East, ready to take part in the celebrations for the 100th anniversary of the signing of the Declaration of Independence. Elizabeth Stanton had written a "Women's Declaration of 1876," which Anthony intended to introduce during Philadelphia's centennial ceremonies. She and Stanton were determined, as they wrote later, "to place on record for the daughters of 1976 the fact that their mothers of 1876 had asserted their equality of rights."

Anthony was denied permission to present the document, but such formalities had never deterred her. On the Fourth of July, she strode through the crowd assembled at Independence Square. Then, ignoring shouts of "Order, Order!" from the military guards, she handed the declaration to the astonished senator on the speaker's platform.

After her unscheduled presentation, she made a speech in front of Philadelphia's Independence Hall. Women asked "no special favors, no special privileges," she said. "We ask justice, we ask equality, we ask that all civil and political rights that belong to the citizens of the United States be guaranteed to us and our daughters forever."

Philadelphians roared their approval of Anthony and the Women's Declaration, but the press did not. In a typical report, the New York *Tribune* asserted that Anthony's action was an example of "the new forms of violence and disregard of order which may accompany the participation of women in active partisan politics."

Active politics, however, were Susan Anthony's life. During the centennial year, she circulated new petitions demanding a woman-suffrage amendment. After gathering 10,000 signatures in 26 states, she presented the petitions to the Senate in 1877. As had so often happened, the women's demands were received with male contempt. "A few [senators] read the petitions . . . with dignity," reported a Washington newspaper, "but the majority seemed intensely conscious of holding something unutterably funny in their hands. . . . The entire Senate presented the appearance of a laughing school practicing side-splitting and ear-extended grins."

As the years passed, Anthony became increasingly exasperated with Lucy Stone's American Woman Suffrage Association, which continued to seek state-by-state support instead of working toward a constitutional amendment. "We have puttered with state rights for 30 years," she fumed,

Spectators assemble in Philadelphia on July 4, 1876, to celebrate the 100th anniversary of the signing of the Declaration of Independence.

"without a foothold except in the territories."

Anthony's beloved sisters Guelma and Hannah had succumbed to tuberculosis in 1873 and 1877, respectively. After their deaths, Anthony had made frequent trips to Rochester to visit her mother, a long-term invalid. When Lucy Read Anthony died in 1880, her daughter, now 60 years old, decided to allow herself time for a monumental project she and Stanton had been longing to undertake: writing a history of the women's movement.

The two old friends worked together as they always had: Anthony organized the material and outlined the book, and Stanton turned it into graceful prose. The authors sent letters to scores of women's-rights activists, asking for reminiscences and anecdotes

London policemen arrest a suffragist demonstrator. British women won the right to vote in 1928, eight years after the victory of their American counterparts.

about the suffrage struggle. In response, they received enthusiastic letters from women and men all over the country—and one short, cold note. It was from Lucy Stone, who said she was "unable" to supply any information. She signed her letter, "Yours with ceaseless regret that any 'wing' of suffragists should attempt to write the history of the other."

Stone's refusal to cooperate on the history did not faze its authors, who produced their first massive volume in an amazing eight months. Published in May 1881, the *History of Woman Suffrage* received a surprisingly warm welcome, both from critics and the public. Typical was the reaction of the Chicago *News*, which had often been hostile to the suffrage movement. The book, said the *News*, was not only "an important literary occurrence," it was a "remarkable event in the history of civilization."

Sales were impressive, both in the United States and England, but the *History* did not make its authors wealthy. They were responsible for production costs, and Anthony had insisted on many expensive illustrations. She also insisted on giving away several thousand copies of the costly book. The *History* was a success, but Anthony and Stanton were as pressed for money as ever. Nevertheless, they immediately started work on the second volume.

Then Anthony received unexpected good news: she had inherited a small fortune—$25,000—from a wealthy Boston woman who had bequeathed an equal amount to Stone and asked that the money be used for "the advancement of the women's rights cause." Filled with "unspeakable gratitude," Anthony went back to work. The second volume of the *History* appeared in 1882; the third, four years later. A record of the women's movement up to 1886, the three-volume work included a thorough history of Lucy Stone's American Association as well as a discussion of arguments that had been used both for and against woman suffrage.

Anthony's inheritance enabled her both to complete the *History* and to take a much-needed vacation. Visiting England with Stanton in 1883, she met the leaders of the British woman-suffrage movement, which faced many of the same problems that confronted the U.S. movement. Like their American counterparts, Anthony discovered, the British suffragists were divided into several camps. As she sailed back to the United States, Anthony got a new idea: She would launch a new, international movement, one that would not only bring together the various factions in each country but that would unite the women of the world.

Once home, Anthony resumed her normal, breakneck routine of traveling, lecturing, writing, presiding over meetings, and circulating petitions. She also found time to lay the groundwork for an international convention, which she scheduled to coincide with the 40th anniversary of the 1848 Seneca Falls Conference. Anthony and her associates mailed out 10,000 invitations to the conference. The response was heartwarming, but one letter of acceptance pleased Anthony far more than any of the others. It was from Lucy Stone. After almost 20 years of separa-

The executive committee of the International Council of Women meets in Washington, D.C., in 1889. Anthony is seated in the front row, third from the left.

Carrie Chapman Catt, Anthony's successor as president of the National-American Woman Suffrage Association, leads a women's rights parade in New York City.

tion, Stone said that she and her American Association members would be pleased to meet with Anthony, Stanton, and their National Association colleagues.

Representatives from 49 countries and 53 American women's organizations appeared in Washington, D.C., for the International Council of Women. It accomplished little of practical value, but it was an important first step, Anthony believed, toward the recognition that the women of the world were allies in the same battle. The meeting also sowed the seeds for a permanent reconciliation of the two major U.S. suffrage organizations: In 1890, Stone's group merged with the association headed by Anthony and Stanton to form the National-American Woman Suffrage Association. Stanton was elected its president.

With a strong organization in place, Anthony now turned her attention back to the West, lecturing in North and South Dakota, Montana, Washington, Idaho, and Wyoming. These pioneer territories were populated by women and men who had long worked side by side as equals, and Anthony was determined that they enter statehood with woman suffrage.

Women had been voting in Wyoming since 1869, but when the territory prepared to enter the Union, Congress had insisted that suffrage be limited to Wyoming's men. Anthony, among others, had been delighted by the Wyoming legislature's response to Congress: "We will remain out of the Union a hundred years rather than come in without woman suffrage."

In July 1890 Anthony was giving a lecture in Madison, South Dakota, when she was handed a telegram from Washington, D.C. Her face blazed with excitement as she read it, first to herself and then to her audience. It said that President Benjamin Harrison had just signed the bill admitting Wyoming to the Union—on its own terms. America had its first woman-suffrage state. Anthony, reported one observer, "spoke as one inspired, while the audience listened for every word, some cheering, others weeping."

The first generation of suffragists was getting old. In 1890, Anthony was 70, Stanton was 75, and many of their colleagues had retired or died. Gradually replacing these veterans was a new wave of dedicated crusaders. Among them were Anna Howard Shaw, a Methodist minister and spellbinding public speaker, and Carrie Chapman Catt, a passionate suffragist from Iowa. In 1893, Catt, under Anthony's tutelage, helped win the campaign for woman suffrage in Colorado. Even with many capable hands to assist her, however, Anthony refused to slow down. At the age of 74 she wrote to a friend, "I am in the midst of as severe a treadmill as I ever experienced, traveling from 50 to 100 miles every day and speaking five or six nights a week."

By 1896—nearly 50 years after the Seneca Falls Convention— woman suffrage had been won in only 4 states: Wyoming, Colorado, Utah, and Idaho. Each year since 1878, a woman-suffrage constitutional amendment had been presented to Congress. Each year it had been ignored or rejected. Despite the monumental efforts of a generation of suffragists, prejudice against women held sway in many areas of society, from religion to marriage to business.

Hostility to the suffrage campaign, always rampant in both major political parties, had been bolstered by the powerful liquor industry. Believing—correctly—that many women voters would try to outlaw alcoholic beverages, alcohol distillers waged an unrelenting campaign to keep women away from the ballot box.

Nonetheless, society had changed, in part through the efforts of women's reform organizations across the nation. Speaking for herself and Stanton, Anthony wrote, "We little dreamed when we began this contest that half a century later we would be compelled to leave the finish of the battle to another generation of women. But our hearts are filled with joy to know that they enter upon this task equipped with a college education, with busi-

Surrounded by mementos and pictures of her colleagues, the tireless Anthony catches up with her correspondence in the early 1900s.

Suffragists from across the nation march with Anna Shaw (in black robe) in a 1912 Manhattan parade. Shaw succeeded Catt as NAWSA president in 1904.

ness experience, with the freely admitted right to speak in public—all of which were denied to women 50 years ago."

When Stanton retired from her post as president of the National-American Association in 1892, Anthony was elected in her place. Active as ever, she continued to dash around the country, traveling to Chicago or California without a moment's hesitation. By the time she reached her 80th birthday, however, she decided it was time to step down. The organization's presidency went to her handpicked successor, Carrie Chapman Catt, whose executive ability she much admired.

In 1902, as Anthony prepared to go to New York to help Stanton celebrate her 87th birthday, she received a telegram from Stanton's daughter. Its message marked the close of a remarkable partnership: "Mother passed away at three o'clock." "It seems impossible that voice is stilled which I have loved to hear for 50 years," Anthony wrote to another friend. "Always I have felt that I must have Mrs. Stanton's opinion of

Suffragists, 20,000 strong, stage a 1915 march in New York City. After decades of such demonstrations, women finally got the vote in 1920.

things before I knew where I stood myself. I am all at sea—but the laws of nature are still going on—with no shadow or turning—what a wonder it is—it goes right on and on—no matter who lives or who dies."

Carrie Chapman Catt, who served as president of the National-American Association for four years, resigned in 1904; with Anthony's support, Anna Shaw became the organization's next president. After getting Shaw elected, Anthony, now 84, headed for Germany and a meeting of the International Council of Women. Tall, thin, and regal in her trademark black silk dress and red silk shawl, she dominated the scene wherever she went. German newsapapers called her "the grand old woman of America," and "Miss Anthony of the world."

Soon after her return to the United States, Anthony went to Portland, Oregon, where she was scheduled to speak at the National-American convention. "Reports have circulated around the country that Miss Anthony was feeble and no longer able to take

No. 27,880.   Entered as second-class matter post office Washington, D. C.

SUFFRAGE PROCLAIMED BY COLBY, WHO SIGNS AT HOME EARLY IN DAY

50 = Year Struggle Ends in Victory for Women

NO CEREMONY IN FINAL ACTION

Secretary Felicitates Leaders; Hails New Era.

Ratification of the nineteenth amendment to the Constitution of the United States, granting suffrage to women, was proclaimed officially to-day by Secretary Colby of the State Department.

The proclamation was signed by Secretary Colby at 8 o'clock this morning at his home, when the certi-

PROCLAMATION ENFRANCHISES WOMEN OF U. S.

Bainbridge Colby, Secretary of State of the United States of America.

To all to whom these presents shall come, greeting:

Know ye, that the Congress of the United States at the first session, Sixty-sixth Congress, begun at Washington on the nineteenth day of May, in the year one thousand nine hundred and nineteen, passed a resolution as follows, to wit:

Joint resolution, proposing an amendment to the Constitution extending the right of suffrage to women.

Resolved by the Senate and House of Representatives of the United States of America in Congress assembled (two-thirds of each House concurring therein), that the following article is proposed as an amendment to the Constitution, which shall be valid to all intents and purposes as part of the Constitution when ratified by the legislatures of three-fourths of the several states.

The New York Times *announces the news that Anthony had not lived to hear: The Constitution's Nineteenth Amendment has been ratified, and American women can vote.*

an active part in suffrage affairs," noted the Portland *Oregonian*, "but when she spoke her first words, an astonished silence fell upon the house. Her voice is more vigorous than that of many women half her age and she speaks with fluency and ease."

In February 1906, Anthony stood through a roaring, 10-minute ovation at a suffrage convention in Baltimore, Maryland, and then made a speech. Its last words were, "I am here for a little time only and then my place will be filled. . . . The fight must not cease; you must see that it does not stop." She ended the final speech of her life with ringing words. "Failure," she said, "is impossible."

But not even the furiously energetic Anthony could go on forever. Soon after the Baltimore convention she was stricken with pneumonia; on March 13, 1906, she died peacefully at her home in Rochester. Anna Shaw, who was with her, later wrote of her final moments, "On the last afternoon of her life, when she had lain quiet for hours, she suddenly began to utter the names of the women who had worked with her, as if in a final roll call.

"Many of them had preceded her into the next world; others were still splendidly active in the work she was laying down. But young or old, living or dead, they all seemed to file past her dying eyes that day in an endless, shadowy review. . . . Then, after lying in silence for a long time with her cheek on my hand, she murmured, 'They are still passing before me—face after face, hundreds and hundreds of them, representing all the efforts of 50 years. I know how hard they have worked. I know the sacrifices they have made. But it has all been worthwhile.' "

Ignoring a howling blizzard, 10,000 silent people lined the streets of Rochester as Anthony's funeral cortege passed. Americans all over the country attended memorial services and read lengthy newspaper tributes to the indomitable crusader. Some editorial writers, however, asserted that the suffrage movement would disappear along with its leader: "Her peculiar views on this question will soon be forgotten," said one. "She was the champion of a lost cause," said another. They were mistaken.

Led by Anthony's dedicated and militant followers, the movement marched on. Particularly effective among the young leaders was Alice Paul, a New Jersey–born activist who was 21 years old when Anthony died. After the election of President Woodrow Wilson in 1912, Paul organized nonstop picketing of the White House, ensuring that Wilson could neither enter nor leave his residence without the sight of the suffragists and their banners. Paul's pickets, along with political pressure and incessant parades, rallies, and speeches staged by women across the nation, finally won the war.

On May 21, 1919, Congress approved the Nineteenth Amendment. "The right of citizens of the United States to vote," it said, "shall not be denied or abridged by the United States or any state on account of sex." The amendment was quickly ratified by 37 states, and in November 1920, America's women cast their first votes. Exactly 100 years after her birth, Susan B. Anthony's dream had come true: Women had become full citizens of the United States.

Honored by her country almost seven decades after her death, Susan B. Anthony is pictured on the U.S. one-dollar coin, first minted in 1979.

FURTHER READING

Anthony, Katharine. *Susan B. Anthony: Her Personal History and Her Era.* New York: Doubleday, 1954.

Buhle, Mari Jo, and Paul Buhle, eds. *The Concise History of Woman Suffrage.* Urbana: University of Illinois Press, 1978.

Cooper, Illene. *Susan B. Anthony.* New York: Franklin Watts, 1984.

Dorr, Rheta Childe. *Susan B. Anthony.* New York: AMS Press, 1970.

DuBois, Ellen Carol, ed. *Elizabeth Cady Stanton/Susan B. Anthony.* New York: Schocken Books, 1981.

————. *Feminism and Suffrage.* Ithaca, NY: Cornell University Press, 1978.

Flexner, Eleanor. *Century of Struggle.* Cambridge: Harvard University Press, 1975.

Harper, Ida Husted. *The Life and Work of Susan B. Anthony.* New York: Arno Press, 1969.

Lutz, Alma. *Susan B. Anthony.* Boston: Beacon Press, 1959.

McHenry, Robert, ed. *Famous American Women: A Biographical Dictionary from Colonial Times to the Present.* New York: Dover, 1980.

Millstein, Beth, and Jeanne Bodin. *We, the American Women: A Documentary History.* Chicago: Science Research Association, 1983.

CHRONOLOGY

Feb. 15, 1820	Susan Brownell Anthony born near Adams, Massachusetts
1826	Moves with her family to Battenville, New York
1837	Attends Philadelphia's Select Seminary for Females
1838	Returns home after economic depression ruins family business
1845	Moves with her parents to Rochester, New York
1846	Appointed headmistress of the "female department" at Canajoharie Academy in upstate New York
1849	Joins Daughters of Temperance; gives first public speech
1851	Meets Elizabeth Cady Stanton
1852	Founds Women's (New York) State Temperance Society
1853–60	Travels across New York State, lecturing on women's property rights
1856–64	Crusades for abolition of slavery
1866	Campaigns for the inclusion of a woman suffrage guarantee in the 14th Amendment
1868	Becomes publisher of woman suffrage newspaper, *The Revolution*
1869	Forms National Woman Suffrage Association
1872	Arrested for voting illegally in Rochester
1881	Publishes, with coauthor Elizabeth Stanton, volume I of *History of Woman Suffrage*
1888	Founds the International Council of Women
1892	Elected president of National-American Woman Suffrage Association
March 13, 1906	Dies in Rochester

INDEX

INDEX

Stanton, Elizabeth Cady, 16, 43, 44, 45, 46,
47, 49, 50, 51, 52, 54, 56, 58, 63, 64, 65,
67, 71, 73, 75, 76, 77, 78, 79, 80, 81, 83,
90, 94, 95, 97, 98, 99, 100, 102
Stanton, Harriot, 51
Stanton, Henry, 50
Stone, Lucy, 46, 47, 56, 75, 76, 81, 83, 84,
88, 95, 96, 97
Stowe, Harriet Beecher, 80
Suffrage
for black men, 14–15, 70, 73, 74, 75, 76,
77, 78, 79, 81
universal, 73
See also Woman suffrage
Suffragists, 14, 15, 19, 64, 75, 77, 84, 99, 100,
105
in England, 97
Susan B. Anthony (Katharine Anthony), 30
Temperance movement, 26, 27, 35, 40, 41,
42, 43, 49, 50, 52–53, 54
Thirteenth Amendment, 69
Train, George Francis, 77, 78, 79
Uncle Tom's Cabin (Stowe), 80
Underground Railroad, 35
U.S. Constitution, 14, 16, 19, 73, 75, 86, 91,
93
U.S. Supreme Court, 91
Utica Evening Standard, 53

Utica Evening Telegraph, 53
Utica Observer, 93
Washington, D.C., 80, 87, 99
Weed, Thurlow, 42
Wilson, Woodrow, 105
Woman suffrage, 14, 44, 45, 71, 73–81, 83,
84, 87, 91, 95, 96, 97, 99, 100, 104, 105
Women's Christian Temperance Union,
54
"Women's Declaration of 1876" (Stanton),
94, 95
Women's National Loyal League, 67, 69
Women's Rights Convention of 1866, 73
Women's rights movement, 43, 44, 45, 46,
50, 53, 54, 56, 58, 59, 61, 64, 65, 66, 71,
73–105
division into factions, 83, 84
and divorce laws, 40, 50, 53, 65, 79
merger of factions, 99
opponents of, 52, 58, 65, 74, 96, 100
and property rights, 54, 55, 57, 59
Women's Rights Society. See American
Equal Rights Society
Women's State (NY) Temperance Society,
50, 52, 53, 54, 55
Woodhull and Claflin's Weekly, 87, 91
Woodhull, Victoria C., 87, 88, 90, 91
Workingwomen's Association, 80

Barbara Weisberg, holder of a master's degree in American Studies from Yale University, is currently a New York City–based writer, producer, and consultant. She works primarily in the area of children's and educational television programming, developing projects for network and cable television and home video. Among the shows she has developed or produced are the series *Livewire* and *Charles in Charge* and a children's special, *Penny Power.*

Matina S. Horner is president of Radcliffe College and associate professor of psychology and social relations at Harvard University. She is best known for her studies of women's motivation, achievement, and personality development. Dr. Horner serves on several national boards and advisory councils, including those of the National Science Foundation, Time Inc., and the Women's Research and Education Institute. She earned her B. A. from Bryn Mawr College and Ph.D. from the University of Michigan, and holds honorary degrees from many colleges and universities, including Mount Holyoke, Smith, Tufts, and the University of Pennsylvania.